THE WILD HISTORY OF THE AMERICAN WEST

THE
OREGON TRAIL
AND THE DARING
JOURNEY WEST BY WAGON

Amy Graham

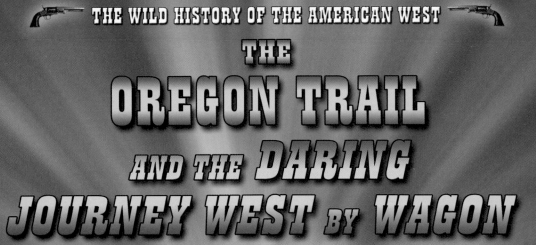

MyReportLinks.com Books

an imprint of

Enslow Publishers, Inc.

Box 398, 40 Industrial Road
Berkeley Heights, NJ 07922
USA

MyReportLinks.com Books, an imprint of Enslow Publishers, Inc. MyReportLinks®
is a registered trademark of Enslow Publishers, Inc.

Library of Congress Cataloging-in-Publication Data

Graham, Amy.
    The Oregon Trail and the daring journey west by wagon / Amy Graham.
        p. cm. — (The wild history of the American West)
    Includes bibliographical references and index.
    ISBN 1-59845-021-2
    1. Pioneers—Oregon National Historic Trail—History—19th century—Juvenile literature.
    2. Pioneers—Oregon National Historic Trail—Social life and customs—19th century—Juvenile
literature. 3. Frontier and pioneer life—Oregon National Historic Trail—Juvenile literature.
    4. Overland journeys to the Pacific—Juvenile literature. 5. Oregon National Historic Trail—
HIstory—Juvenile literature. I. Title. II. Series.
    F597.G73 2006
    917.804'2—dc22

                                2005031088

Printed in the United States of America

10 9 8 7 6 5 4 3 2 1

To Our Readers:
Through the purchase of this book, you and your library gain access to the Report Links that specifically
back up this book.
The Publisher will provide access to the Report Links that back up this book and will keep these Report
Links up to date on **www.myreportlinks.com** for five years from the book's first publication date.
We have done our best to make sure all Internet addresses in this book were active and appropriate when
we went to press. However, the author and the Publisher have no control over, and assume no liability
for, the material available on those Internet sites or on other Web sites they may link to.
The usage of the MyReportLinks.com Books Web site is subject to the terms and conditions stated on the
Usage Policy Statement on **www.myreportlinks.com.**
A password may be required to access the Report Links that back up this book. The password is found
on the bottom of page 4 of this book.
Any comments or suggestions can be sent by e-mail to comments@myreportlinks.com or to the address
on the back cover.

Photo Credits: American Studies at the University of Virginia, p. 109; © American Indians of the
Pacific Northwest, p. 105; © Corel Corporation, pp. 3 (top left), 12–13, 42–43, 48–49, 53, 68–69, 75,
77, 97; © 1995 PhotoDisc, p. 20–21; © 1998 KERA, p. 39; © Paul Halsall June 1998, p. 31; © The
Sacramento Bee, p. 58; © 2003 by Boettcher/Trinklein Inc., pp. 10, 87; © 2004–05 PBS/WGBH, pp. 22,
35, 82, 94, 96; © 2005 American History Magazine, p. 84; © 2005 by Susanne "Sam" Behling, p. 55;
© 2005 Washington State Historical Society, p. 113; © 2005 Wild West Magazine, p. 57; © 2006 History
Ink, p. 33; Courtesy of Dictionary of American Portraits, by Dover Publications, Inc., in 1967, pp. 32, 34;
End of the Oregon Trail Interpretive Center © 2004, 2005, pp. 65, 73; Enslow Publishers, Inc., p. 5;
Library of Congress, pp. 1, 3 (top right), 7 (dog and man panning for gold, Indian chief), 15, 24, 40, 62,
71, 80, 85, 89, 92, 99, 101, 111, 115; Michael W. Kidd, Summer 1996, p. 51; MyReportLinks.com Books,
p. 4; National Park Service, pp. 17, 18, 79, 104, 117; Nebraska State Historical Society, p. 36;
Photos.com, pp. 6, 7 (background, buffalo, wagon train), 107; Robert L. Munkres, p. 60; Stephenie Flora,
p. 28; The Mariners' Museum, p. 30; University of Washington Libraries, p. 100.

Cover: Library of Congress

Cover Description: Silhouetted from the painting "Emigrants Crossing the Plains," painted by Felix
Octavius Carr Darley and engraved by Henry Bryan Hall.

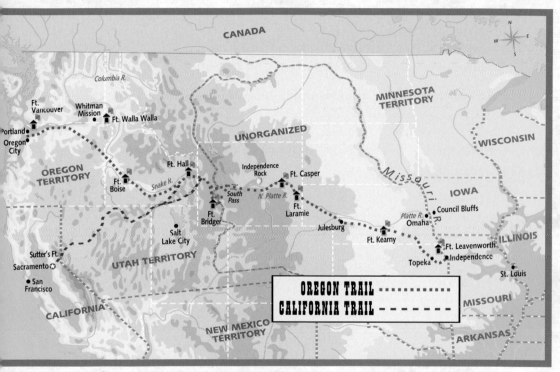

▲ A map of the Oregon and California trails.

▷ **1792**—American Robert Gray discovers the mouth of the Columbia River.

▷ **1803**—United States purchases the Louisiana Territory from France.

▷ **1804**—President Thomas Jefferson sends Lewis and Clark to explore the territory west of the Mississippi River.

▷ **1805**—Lewis and Clark reach Oregon and the shores of the Pacific Ocean.

▷ **1811**—Pacific Fur Company builds a fur trading fort, named Astoria, in Oregon Country.

▷ **1812**—Robert Stuart of the Pacific Fur Company finds South Pass through the Rockies.

—War of 1812 breaks out between United States and Great Britain.

▷ **1818**—United States and Great Britain agree to jointly occupy Oregon Country.

▷ **1836**—Marcus and Narcissa Whitman begin a mission in Oregon for the Cayuse people.

▷ **1837**—American banks fail and wages drop, causing the Panic of 1837.

▷ **1840**—Joel Walker and family become the first American settlers to arrive in Oregon.

▷ **1841**—Bidwell-Bartleson party becomes first wagon train to go overland.

▷ **1843**—A group of one thousand pioneers heads to Oregon. This is called the Great Migration.

▷ **1846**—British and Americans agree to divide the Oregon country at the 49th parallel.

—Donner Party is trapped in the Sierra Nevada Mountains.

—Brigham Young leads Mormons to resettle in Great Salt Lake Valley.

▷ **1848**—Gold is discovered at Sutter's Mill in California.

—Mexican War ends: United States acquires California, the Southwest, and Texas.

—Oregon becomes a United States territory.

—United States builds Fort Kearny in Nebraska to protect emigrants from hostile Indians.

▷ **1849**—First wave of gold miners from the United States goes west to California.

—Cholera epidemic spreads along the Oregon Trail.

▷ **1850**—California gains statehood.

—Congress passes the Donation Land Claim Act, which provides free land to emigrants.

▷ **1854**—Emigrants and soldiers are massacred by American Indians in two separate incidents.

▷ **1855**—American soldiers destroy a Sioux Indian village in the Battle of Blue Water.

▷ **1859**—Oregon becomes the thirty-third state of the Union.

▷ **1861**—Western Union completes telegraph lines from coast to coast.

▷ **1869**—Transcontinental Railroad, from Omaha, northeast to Sacramento, California, is completed.

▷ **1877**—Nez Percé tribe attempts to flee the United States and go to Canada to escape life on a reservation.

▷ **1883**—Northern Pacific Railroad completes a line to Portland, Oregon.

Chapter 1 ▶

TRIALS AND ADVENTURES OF THE PIONEERS

Just two hundred years ago, the American West was a vast wilderness. It was home to millions of buffalo and many nations of American Indians. Over the next fifty years, the United States grabbed up huge tracts of land—the Louisiana Territory, Texas, Oregon Country, and California. Americans went to settle in these new places. The first Americans to venture west were bold and daring pioneers. They braved bad weather, rough trails, and on rare occasions, attacks by hostile Indians. Some died along the way: sick, starving, or cold. The risks of going west were considerable. Yet most of the settlers succeeded in building better lives for themselves on the frontier. The pioneers took part in a great migration of people. Over the course of a few decades, hundreds of thousands of people went west in covered wagons along the Oregon Trail. Many of the pioneers realized they were making history. They recorded their thoughts and experiences in diaries. Here are some of their stories:

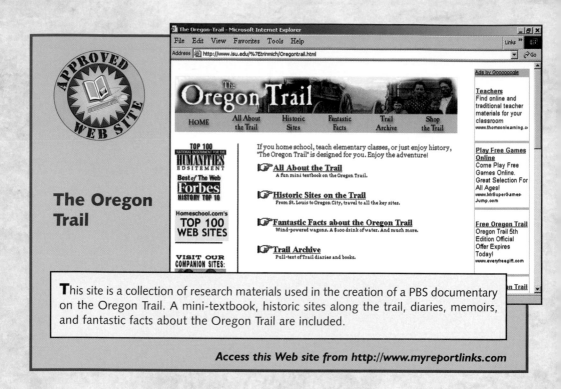

APPROVED WEB SITE

The Oregon Trail

This site is a collection of research materials used in the creation of a PBS documentary on the Oregon Trail. A mini-textbook, historic sites along the trail, diaries, memoirs, and fantastic facts about the Oregon Trail are included.

Access this Web site from http://www.myreportlinks.com

▶ A Humanitarian Journey

Marcus Whitman was looking for a way to make the world a better place. He had resolved to start a mission to help modernize American Indians and convert them to Christianity. And so, in 1835, the doctor and Presbyterian Church elder joined a company of merchants headed west into Indian Territory. The merchants' wagons were loaded with provisions to trade with fur trappers. The merchants would trade their supplies for furs to sell back east. The wagon train crossed the Missouri River and set out upon the great rolling prairie. The wide sky stretched above them in all directions. The terrain grew drier as the wagons approached the great Rocky Mountains. On the other side of these mountains lay Dr. Whitman's destination: the Oregon Country. Oregon Country was a vast territory in the Pacific Northwest. It lay west of the Rockies, between the Russian territory of Alaska and Mexico's California. In the 1830s, the Oregon Country was not yet American soil. The British and Americans jointly occupied it. Whitman's travels that year took him through a country few white people had ever seen. Excited by his dreams of starting a mission, he returned home to New York to convince others to join him.

While back east, he met and married a young woman named Narcissa Prentiss. Marcus and Narcissa Whitman spent their honeymoon in a covered wagon headed west. Another missionary couple, Henry Spalding and his wife, Eliza, traveled with them. Narcissa Whitman and Eliza Spalding became the first white women to cross the Rocky Mountains. These pioneering women proved to Americans that the West was not just for young men. Their migration opened the door for other families to come west. The Whitmans also established that it was possible to take a covered wagon across the Rockies. Though their wagon served them well, it did not make it the entire way. They abandoned it in what is now Idaho when

A covered wagon moving along the path of the Oregon Trail near Fort Kearny, Nebraska. The Whitmans headed out toward the Rocky Mountains in a covered wagon in hopes of working to benefit American Indians as missionaries.

trappers told them they would not be able to take it past Fort Boise.

Mission at Waiilatpu

After several months of traveling, the Whitman and Spalding party reached a British outpost in present-day Washington: Fort Walla Walla. They decided to look no further. Fort Walla Walla was a fur trading post owned by the Hudson's Bay Company. It served as a trading spot for the company's fur trappers and American Indians. The Whitmans established their mission nearby at a spot called Waiilatpu. Waiilatpu means "Place of Rye Grass." The mission served several small villages of Cayuse Indians. The Whitmans started a school for the Cayuse children. They planted extensive vegetable gardens. They built a mill to grind wheat into flour. Henry and Eliza Spalding began their mission among the Nez Percé Indians.

The Whitmans soon found that the growing number of pioneers also needed their help. Inspired by the Whitmans and other adventurers, by the 1840s, more determined families were moving west to the Oregon Country. By the time the pioneers reached Fort Walla Walla, many were hungry, tired, and in need of fresh supplies. The nearby Whitman mission offered food and shelter to the weary travelers. The year 1844 was an especially hard one for the wagon trains. Snow had

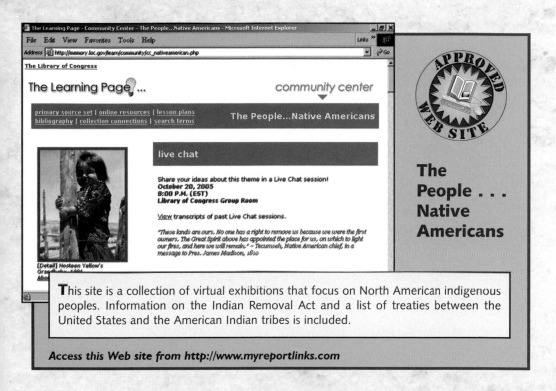

The
People . . .
Native
Americans

This site is a collection of virtual exhibitions that focus on North American indigenous peoples. Information on the Indian Removal Act and a list of treaties between the United States and the American Indian tribes is included.

Access this Web site from http://www.myreportlinks.com

covered the Blue Mountains by the time they arrived in late October. The Whitmans took in many people for the winter. In a letter home to her parents, Narcissa wrote:

> It is expected that there are more than five hundred souls back in the snow and mountains. Among the number is an orphan family of seven children, the youngest an infant born on the way, whose parents have both died since they left the States. Application has been made for us to take them, as they have not a relative in their company. What we shall do I cannot say; we cannot see them suffer, if the Lord casts them upon us. He will give us His grace and strength to do our duty to them.[1]

The Whitmans agreed to adopt the orphans (the Sager children) when they arrived.

▶ Medicine or Poison?

Marcus Whitman was also a medical doctor. He treated both pioneers and American Indians. The Cayuse Indians had their own traditional doctors called medicine men. A medicine man was an important figure in Cayuse society. A good medicine man was a powerful and honored person in the tribe. Yet it was a risky career. According to Cayuse tradition, a tribe member could kill a medicine man in revenge for dispensing bad medicine.[2] This tradition would play an important role in the tragedy at Waiilatpu.

Trouble arrived when a wagon train is believed to have brought measles into the mission in 1847. Measles was a common childhood disease in the United States in those days. The children who recovered could resist measles if they were exposed to it again. At Waiilatpu, measles quickly infected the children and spread to the Cayuse Indians. Most of the children at the mission quickly recovered under Dr. Whitman's care. The Cayuse tribes, however, were devastated. They had never encountered measles and had no immunity to the illness. The disease killed half of the tribe within a few weeks.

The remaining Cayuse were frightened and grief stricken. Some came to the conclusion that Dr. Whitman was poisoning them.[3] In a revenge attack, a group of Cayuse men brutally murdered fourteen people at the mission. Dr. Whitman and his wife, as well as two of their adopted children, were among the dead. The third child died while being held captive. Another fifty-four women and children were held hostage for weeks. Two years later, a handful of Cayuse turned themselves in, claiming they were responsible for the killings. A jury of Oregon City settlers tried

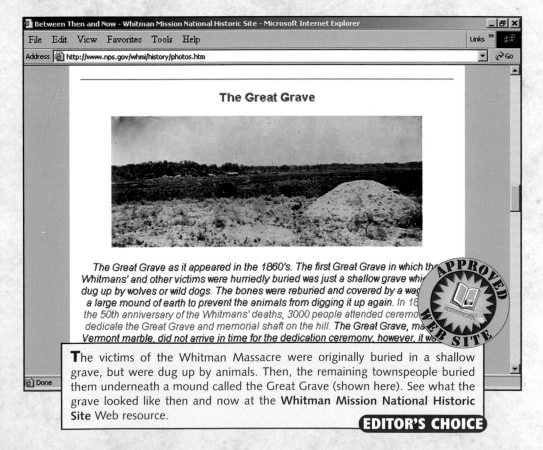

The Great Grave

The Great Grave as it appeared in the 1860's. The first Great Grave in which the Whitmans' and other victims were hurriedly buried was just a shallow grave which dug up by wolves or wild dogs. The bones were reburied and covered by a wag a large mound of earth to prevent the animals from digging it up again. In 18 the 50th anniversary of the Whitmans' deaths, 3000 people attended ceremo dedicate the Great Grave and memorial shaft on the hill. The Great Grave, ma Vermont marble, did not arrive in time for the dedication ceremony, however, it wa

The victims of the Whitman Massacre were originally buried in a shallow grave, but were dug up by animals. Then, the remaining townspeople buried them underneath a mound called the Great Grave (shown here). See what the grave looked like then and now at the **Whitman Mission National Historic Site** Web resource.

EDITOR'S CHOICE

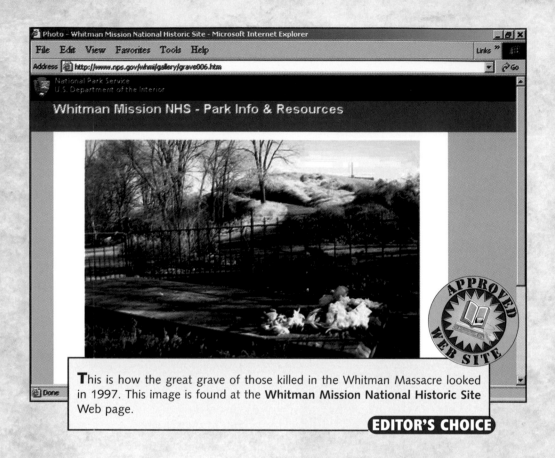

Photo - Whitman Mission National Historic Site - Microsoft Internet Explorer

File   Edit   View   Favorites   Tools   Help   Links »

Address http://www.nps.gov/whmi/gallery/grave006.htm   Go

National Park Service
U.S. Department of the Interior

Whitman Mission NHS - Park Info & Resources

This is how the great grave of those killed in the Whitman Massacre looked in 1997. This image is found at the **Whitman Mission National Historic Site** Web page.

Done

EDITOR'S CHOICE

the men and found them guilty beyond a doubt. Hundreds of settlers turned out to watch the men hanged.

The Whitman massacre was just one example of the woes that occurred when the pioneer and American Indian cultures clashed. In similar misunderstandings, pioneers murdered many American Indians. Within a few decades, American pioneers had established their rule over the Oregon Country. American Indians were forced to sign treaties, agreeing to move onto reservations.

The Donner Party: Snowbound

After the Whitman massacre, pioneers grew fearful of American Indian attacks, but they had many other things to worry about, too. In the high elevations of the western mountains, the snow begins falling in the early autumn. Most of the settlers crossed the mountains before the snow began to pile up. If they reached the mountains too late in the season, snowdrifts of 30 to 40 feet could block their way. They would be trapped in the wilderness without food to last through the winter. One infamous group of settlers suffered this very fate. The tragic story of the Donner Party is easily the most famous and most horrible of any tale of emigrants bound for the West.

George Donner led an emigrant wagon train of about ninety people along the Oregon Trail in 1846. They were bound for California, which was then a territory of Mexico. Many Americans settled there, as they rightly believed it would soon become part of the United States. Emigrants bound for California usually followed the Oregon Trail as far as Fort Hall in present-day Idaho. At Fort Hall, they would take the California Trail that led on to San Francisco. But not the Donner Party: They took a different route. Following the advice of a guide named Lansford Hastings, they abandoned the trail and bushwhacked through Wyoming, Utah, and Nevada. Hastings had

Modern paved roads make it easy to get through Donner Pass. Still, at certain times of the year, the weather can make it a treacherous journey.

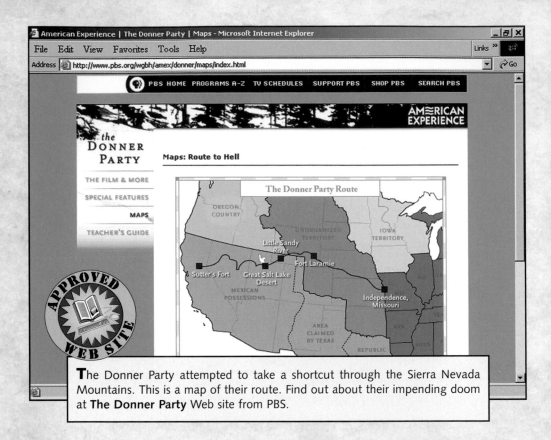

Address http://www.pbs.org/wgbh/amex/donner/maps/index.html

The Donner Party Route

OREGON
COUNTRY

UNORGANIZED
TERRITORY

IOWA
TERRITORY

Little Sandy
River

Fort Laramie

Sutter's Fort   Great Salt Lake
Desert

MEXICAN
POSSESSIONS

Independence,
Missouri

AREA
CLAIMED
BY TEXAS

REPUBLIC

The Donner Party attempted to take a shortcut through the Sierra Nevada Mountains. This is a map of their route. Find out about their impending doom at **The Donner Party** Web site from PBS.

written about the "shortcut" in his guidebook, *The Emigrants' Guide to Oregon and California.*

This decision turned out to be a horrible error. Instead of saving time, the cutoff took them six weeks longer than usual. They had to slash their way through thick brush and climb steep hills. Worst of all, the path took them across the bleak salt desert of Utah. By day, the desert heat was intense. There was no grass or water for over seventy miles. Many of their animals died of exhaustion and thirst.

When the party reached the Sierra Nevada Mountains of California in late October, snow had already begun to fall. When the snow reached the axles of their wagons, they abandoned them. They pressed on by foot through the waist-deep snow. But the snow was falling fast, and the exhausted party gave up hope. They retreated to the shores of a lake where they had seen the remains of some old cabins. Even here the snow already lay a foot deep. With few remaining provisions, they resolved themselves to spending months in the wilderness. The party fixed up the rough log cabins and covered them with animal hides. Butchering their few remaining oxen and horses, they froze the meat so it would last. The men tried hunting and fishing, but had limited success.

Lovina Graves, a member of the Donner Party, was just a small child that winter. She later reminisced about seeing fish moving beneath the ice, but being unable to catch them.[4] When their food supplies ran out, the emigrants boiled the animal hides that covered their cabins. The result was a pot full of glue that was hard to eat and gave them little energy. Weak from lack of food, they had a hard time gathering wood for fires.

In mid-December, fifteen desperate men and women set out over the mountains in a last attempt to go for help. They went on snowshoes they had fashioned from tree branches. Snow and

▲ This photo was taken at Donner Lake in 1866. The stumps of trees cut down by the Donner Party were still there.

rain plagued them on their trip. They quickly consumed their remaining dried beef and coffee. Raving and delirious with weakness, one by one they died of exposure and starvation. One man, Franklin Graves, grew too weak to go on. According to some accounts, the dying Mr. Graves told his daughters to fend off starvation by using his body for food.[5] After a month, five women and two men made it to safety. While they recovered, they made plans to rescue the family and friends still trapped in the mountains. The final rescue group arrived in mid-April, after several earlier attempts. To reach the trapped party, they had floundered across the mountains through ten feet of snow. The rescuers found some survivors. Nearly half of the party had perished. Hungry wolves had scavenged the snowy graves. Here, too, some people, faced with starving to death, had resorted to eating their dead companions.

The horrifying story spread like wildfire among the emigrants. The suffering of the Donner Party served as a warning. First, beware of shortcuts. Second, move quickly. Wagon trains needed to leave as early in the spring as possible to avoid snow. In future years, Californians organized relief efforts to help stragglers cross the mountains safely. The lesson for some would-be emigrants was to stay safely at home. One survivor, Miss Mary Ann Graves, was just nineteen when her family set out with the Donner Party. She arrived in California an orphan. In a letter to friends she wrote: "I will now give you some good and friendly advice. Stay at home,—you are in a good place, where, if sick, you are not in danger of starving to death."[6] From her advice, it is clear to see she did not find her new home in California worth the dear price she paid.

Chapter 2 ▶

EARLY DAYS OF THE OREGON COUNTRY

The area of the Oregon Country stretched from the present-day state of Oregon all the way north to Alaska. American Indians lived in Oregon for thousands of years prior to the pioneers' arrival. It was not until the eighteenth century that the first non-Indians came to the Pacific Coast of Oregon. These explorers found the shores inhabited by the Chinook people. Huge cedar trees grew to towering heights in the cool, rainy climate. The Chinook hollowed out cedar logs to make canoes. They built their homes from cedar planks. The Chinook used cedar bark to make baskets, fishing nets, and mats. They hunted animals and gathered wild plants and berries to eat, but salmon was the mainstay of their diet. So many salmon swam up river in the spring that the tribes could catch enough in their nets to feed themselves all year long. To preserve the fish, they hung the salmon on racks to dry in the sun.

One thing the Chinook had not done was to clear the land for farming. Neither had other

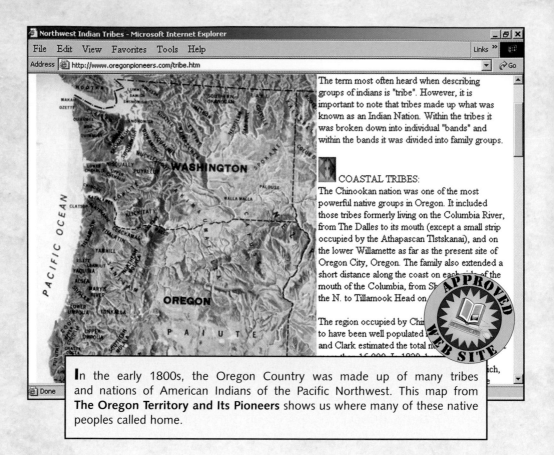

Northwest Indian Tribes - Microsoft Internet Explorer

File   Edit   View   Favorites   Tools   Help   Links »

Address http://www.oregonpioneers.com/tribe.htm   Go

The term most often heard when describing groups of indians is "tribe". However, it is important to note that tribes made up what was known as an Indian Nation. Within the tribes it was broken down into individual "bands" and within the bands it was divided into family groups.

COASTAL TRIBES:
The Chinookan nation was one of the most powerful native groups in Oregon. It included those tribes formerly living on the Columbia River, from The Dalles to its mouth (except a small strip occupied by the Athapascan Tlstskanai), and on the lower Willamette as far as the present site of Oregon City, Oregon. The family also extended a short distance along the coast on each side of the mouth of the Columbia, from S[...] the N. to Tillamook Head on [...]

The region occupied by Chi[...] to have been well populated [...] and Clark estimated the total n[...]

In the early 1800s, the Oregon Country was made up of many tribes and nations of American Indians of the Pacific Northwest. This map from **The Oregon Territory and Its Pioneers** shows us where many of these native peoples called home.

American Indians. Many American Indians moved their villages place to place, following the animals they hunted. This way of living was foreign to the Europeans. As a result, they did not recognize that the land belonged to the American Indians.[1] Instead, they saw an unclaimed wilderness.

▶ Old World Explorers Find the Americas

The earliest European explorers to see America were searching for a new route to Asia. China was a wealthy land that could trade silk, tea, and spices. The merchants of Europe were eager to trade with China and the Spice Islands. However, getting there and back took a long time. Ships had to sail south around Africa's Cape Horn and then across the Indian Ocean. A more direct route would save a lot of time and money. So the Europeans sent explorers west across the Atlantic in search of a new way to Asia. No one knew what lay on the other side of the Atlantic Ocean.

Christopher Columbus landed in the Americas in 1492. He mistook it for a part of Asia called the Indies. That is why he called the people he met Indians. After a little more exploration, many Europeans soon understood Columbus had visited a new land: the Americas.

Sea Route to Asia?

The Americas stood in the way of a route to Asia. Explorers now had a new quest. They searched for a way to sail their ships through the Americas. Sailors told stories of a Northwest Passage running through North America. French and English ships explored every nook and cranny of the Atlantic coastline. They searched for a river that would take them west. The St. Lawrence River looked promising, but they found it went no farther west than the Great Lakes. The Spanish searched for a similar passageway through Central and South America.

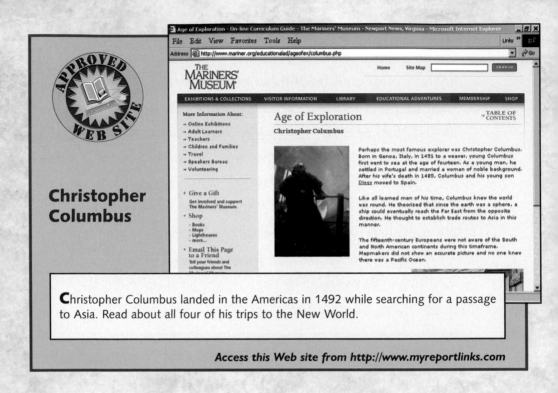

Christopher
Columbus

Age of Exploration
Christopher Columbus

Perhaps the most famous explorer was Christopher Columbus. Born in Genoa, Italy, in 1451 to a weaver, young Columbus first went to sea at the age of fourteen. As a young man, he settled in Portugal and married a woman of noble background. After his wife's death in 1485, Columbus and his young son Diego moved to Spain.

Like all learned men of his time, Columbus knew the world was round. He theorized that since the earth was a sphere, a ship could eventually reach the Far East from the opposite direction. He thought to establish trade routes to Asia in this manner.

The fifteenth-century Europeans were not aware of the South and North American continents during this timeframe. Mapmakers did not show an accurate picture and no one knew there was a Pacific Ocean.

Christopher Columbus landed in the Americas in 1492 while searching for a passage to Asia. Read about all four of his trips to the New World.

Access this Web site from http://www.myreportlinks.com

Ferdinand Magellan was a Portuguese sea captain. He believed it was possible to get to Asia by sailing west. When he could not get his own country to send him, he turned to the neighboring country of Spain. The Spanish supported his ideas, though they seemed crazy to most people at the time. Magellan became the first person to reach the Pacific Ocean by sailing west from Europe. His travels took him around the tip of South America, close to the frigid waters around Antarctica. The route is now known as the Strait of Magellan. His discovery opened the door to Spanish exploration of the Americas. In time, Spain controlled much of the Pacific coastline of the Americas, including present-day Mexico and California. Spain also claimed to own the Pacific Northwest. In 1819, they ceded this claim to the United States.

It took hundreds of years for mapmakers to make an accurate map of the Americas. Vitus Bering, a sea captain for the Russian Navy, answered one of the perplexing questions of his time. People wondered if North America and Asia were part of the same continent. Bering sailed his ship between Russia and present-day Alaska in 1728. The Bering Strait, named after the captain, was final proof that North America was a separate continent from Asia.[2] Bering returned to entertain the tsar of Russia with tales of the many fur

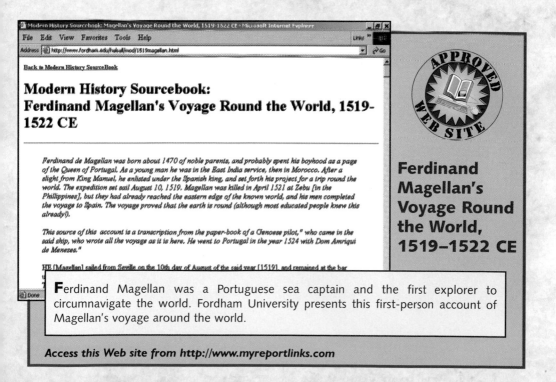

Ferdinand Magellan was a Portuguese sea captain and the first explorer to circumnavigate the world. Fordham University presents this first-person account of Magellan's voyage around the world.

Access this Web site from http://www.myreportlinks.com

animals in the region. The tsar soon established a Russian American territory in present-day Alaska. The Russians were eager to get a foothold in the fur-rich Americas.

The fur market was booming. Before the discovery of synthetic materials like polyester and fleece, people used animal fur to make warm, water-resistant hats, coats, and gloves. Russian merchants traded the furs with China, in exchange for tea. In the 1820s, Russia gave up any claims to the Oregon Country. The boundary between Russia's American territory and the Oregon Country was set at a line on the map called 54°40′. Fifty-four forty is a measurement called the latitude. Latitude marks the distance north from the equator. The equator is another line that runs around the center of the earth. The Russians retained a firm hold in America until 1876, when they sold Alaska to the United States.

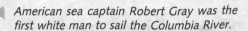

American sea captain Robert Gray was the first white man to sail the Columbia River.

▶ Who Would Win Oregon?

With Russia and Spain out of the running, the fight for Oregon was down to the Americans and the British. The British-owned Hudson's Bay Company had built Fort Vancouver, a large fur trading post in the Oregon Country. The company owned a chain of smaller trading forts throughout the country. It had formed trading partnerships with the American Indians there. The United States' claim to the area was weaker. American sea captain Robert Gray had happened across the

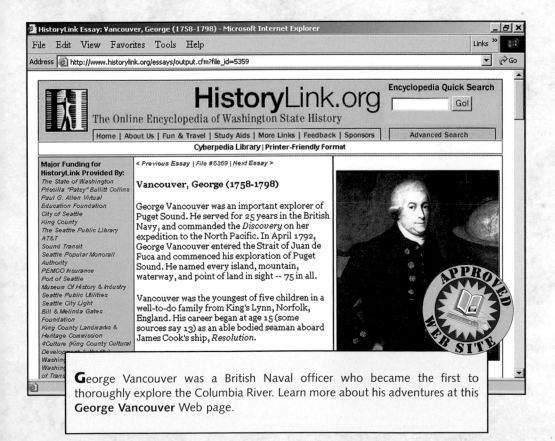

George Vancouver was a British Naval officer who became the first to thoroughly explore the Columbia River. Learn more about his adventures at this **George Vancouver** Web page.

wide mouth of the Columbia River in 1792. Gray's discovery meant that America could claim to own the Pacific Northwest. Yet Gray had not stopped to explore the Columbia. He traded for beaver and otter pelts with the American Indians he met there and then sailed on. It was a British sea captain, George Vancouver, who had first explored the Columbia after hearing of Gray's discovery.[3]

In 1803, the United States purchased the Louisiana Territory from France. President Thomas Jefferson sent a party of men to explore the Louisiana Purchase. The president wanted a full report on the natural treasures of the territory. He also wanted to know if there was a water route that went west to the Pacific Ocean. Jefferson chose Meriwether Lewis and William Clark to lead the expedition. Lewis and Clark and their Corps of Discovery traveled west from 1804 to 1806. They went up the Missouri River and continued overland. They pushed across

John Jacob Astor was a wealthy fur trader and real estate tycoon.

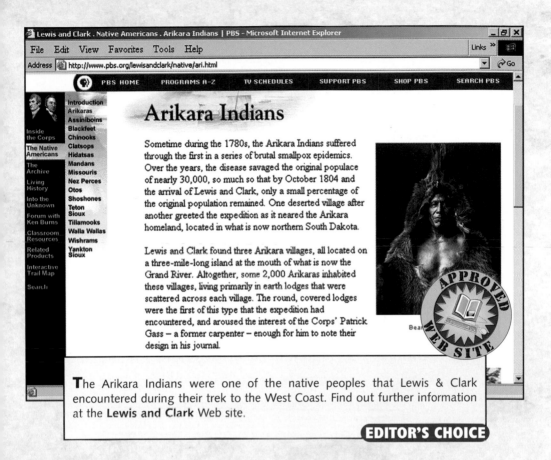

Lewis and Clark . Native Americans . Arikara Indians | PBS - Microsoft Internet Explorer

File Edit View Favorites Tools Help

Address http://www.pbs.org/lewisandclark/native/ari.html

PBS HOME   PROGRAMS A-Z   TV SCHEDULES   SUPPORT PBS   SHOP PBS   SEARCH PBS

Inside the Corps
The Native Americans
The Archive
Living History
Into the Unknown
Forum with Ken Burns
Classroom Resources
Related Products
Interactive Trail Map
Search

Introduction
Arikaras
Assiniboins
Blackfeet
Chinooks
Clatsops
Hidatsas
Mandans
Missouris
Nez Perces
Otos
Shoshones
Teton Sioux
Tillamooks
Walla Wallas
Wishrams
Yankton Sioux

Arikara Indians

Sometime during the 1780s, the Arikara Indians suffered through the first in a series of brutal smallpox epidemics. Over the years, the disease savaged the original populace of nearly 30,000, so much so that by October 1804 and the arrival of Lewis and Clark, only a small percentage of the original population remained. One deserted village after another greeted the expedition as it neared the Arikara homeland, located in what is now northern South Dakota.

Lewis and Clark found three Arikara villages, all located on a three-mile-long island at the mouth of what is now the Grand River. Altogether, some 2,000 Arikaras inhabited these villages, living primarily in earth lodges that were scattered across each village. The round, covered lodges were the first of this type that the expedition had encountered, and aroused the interest of the Corps' Patrick Gass – a former carpenter – enough for him to note their design in his journal.

APPROVED WEB SITE

The Arikara Indians were one of the native peoples that Lewis & Clark encountered during their trek to the West Coast. Find out further information at the **Lewis and Clark** Web site.

EDITOR'S CHOICE

the Rockies and on to the mouth of the Columbia River. They became the first Americans to travel overland to the Pacific. Their pioneering travels greatly improved the United States' claim to the Oregon Country.

The Fur Trade

Lewis and Clark had returned from the West with stories of bountiful wildlife. Americans were eager to establish themselves in the fur trade. The British were making huge profits in

North America. Animal pelts were in high demand in Europe, where they had long since killed off their own stocks of fur animals. The waterproof pelts of American beavers were especially popular. One American, John Jacob Astor, made a fortune in the fur trade. He owned the American Fur Company, based out of New York and northern Michigan. His success led him to create the Pacific Fur Company. Astor was the first American to compete with the British traders in the Pacific Northwest. Astor's men went to Oregon in 1810. Some traveled on a three-masted ship, the *Tonquin,* around the southern tip of South America. Other members of Astor's company became some of the first to

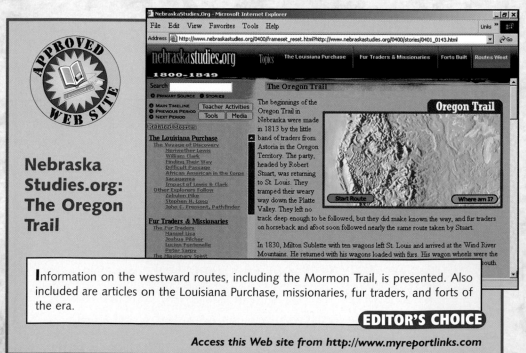

**Nebraska
Studies.org:
The Oregon
Trail**

Information on the westward routes, including the Mormon Trail, is presented. Also included are articles on the Louisiana Purchase, missionaries, fur traders, and forts of the era.

EDITOR'S CHOICE

Access this Web site from http://www.myreportlinks.com

travel overland to the Pacific. They built a trading fort near the Columbia River and named it Astoria. The fort paved the way for the future American settlement of Oregon.

Astor envisioned building trading forts across North America. Other American companies had different ideas. The young frontier town of St. Louis, Missouri, was becoming a hot spot in the fur trade. William H. Ashley was a prominent St. Louis businessman who entered the fur trade in the 1820s. Ashley sent his men overland to trap in the Rocky Mountains. They followed the banks of the Platte River through Nebraska and into Wyoming. Instead of swapping their furs at a fort, Ashley's trappers met him at an annual rendezvous in the West. Merchants brought supply wagons along the Platte River route to the rendezvous. This route was the beginning of the overland trail to Oregon and California.

War of 1812

In 1812, the United States was still a young country struggling to gain respect from Europe. It had only been independent from Great Britain for thirty-six years. The British, in particular, gave the United States a hard time. The British Royal Navy desperately needed sailors to fight in the war against Napoléon, the leader of France. To build their forces, the British Navy routinely captured ships at sea. Through brute force, they drafted any men on board to become British seamen. They captured thousands of Americans in this manner.

Americans were outraged at the practice. To strike back, the United States Congress passed the Embargo Act in 1807. It outlawed any trade with Europe. Of course, trade goes two ways. America's own economy was badly hurt. Tensions built between the Americans and the British. In 1812, war broke out between the two countries. Americans hoped to conquer part of British-controlled Canada. Yet as the war developed, neither side gained much ground. The Pacific Fur Company fled Astoria, leaving the area to the British.

The war was resolved on Christmas Day, December 25, 1814. British and Americans signed a peace treaty in the Belgian city of Ghent. Both countries agreed to stop fighting and to respect each other's boundaries. The issue of who owned the Oregon Country was not addressed. In 1818, America and Great Britain agreed to share Oregon. They would jointly occupy the land in a peaceful manner.

A Growing Country

In the early 1800s, the United States owned a fraction of the land it does today. Americans primarily lived in cities and towns up and down the Atlantic coast. A first wave of pioneers had ventured across the Appalachian Mountains to settle in Tennessee and Kentucky. Much of the continent remained a wilderness. Few Americans lived farther west than the Missouri River.

Americans had big plans for their democracy. They hoped to stretch the border of the country all the way across the continent to the Pacific Ocean. With courage and hard work, the pioneers meant to tame the wilderness and claim it for America. They also wanted to make new and better lives for themselves. "Oregon Fever" infected thousands of Americans between 1840 and 1860. They sold their homes, packed up their belongings, and bought a covered wagon. These pioneers were

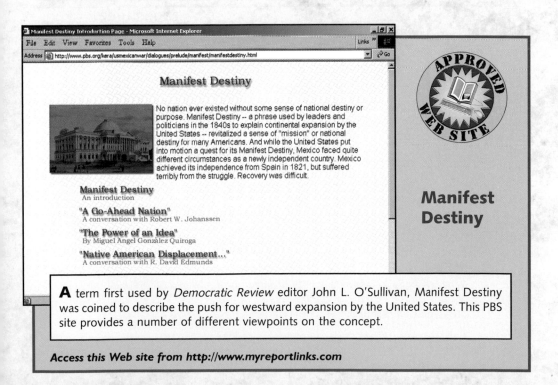

A term first used by *Democratic Review* editor John L. O'Sullivan, Manifest Destiny was coined to describe the push for westward expansion by the United States. This PBS site provides a number of different viewpoints on the concept.

Access this Web site from http://www.myreportlinks.com

▲ James Knox Polk was the eleventh president of the United States. He is most well-known for expanding the borders of the country to the northwest and southwest. This painting was originally done by artist Albert Newsam.

also called emigrants. Emigrants are people who leave their country to live elsewhere. These emigrants left the United States to settle on the western frontier.

The emigrants shed many a tear while saying their good-byes. It was unlikely that they would ever again see the family and friends they left behind. It was a long and difficult trip overland to Oregon. The pioneers followed the rough Oregon Trail, which was sometimes little more than faint wagon ruts. It carried the pioneers across the wide-open prairies, dry deserts, and rugged mountains. The trail began at the Missouri River. Its end was the Willamette Valley of Oregon. Oregon was said to be a land of milk and honey. The soil was fertile. Water was plentiful. It was rumored to be a farmer's paradise.

Manifest Destiny

In the mid-1800s, Americans were excited about a new idea. They called the idea Manifest Destiny. A newspaperman named John O'Sullivan coined the phrase in 1845. As more Americans were born each year, the country would need more land, he argued. Americans had a God-given responsibility. It was their duty to spread democracy as they expanded. A patriotic fever burned in the United States. Americans took their duty seriously and moved west, making America's claim to the Oregon

The Willamette River valley was the final stop on the Oregon Trail.

Country stronger. Every fall, more emigrants arrived from the States. The British claim grew weaker as time wore on. The fur trade was a dying industry. Their claim to Oregon depended on their trading posts.

James K. Polk

In 1845, the eleventh president of the United States took office. President James K. Polk was a Democrat from Tennessee. He was a firm believer in Manifest Destiny. Polk gained more territory for the United States than any other president since Jefferson's Louisiana Purchase. During his term, the Oregon issue was settled once and for all. In June 1846, Great Britain and the United States agreed to split the Oregon Country. Some Americans felt entitled to the entire Oregon Country, all the way to the Alaskan border. Around the streets of America, people chanted "54° 40' or fight!" They wanted the United States to own all the way to the 54° 40' latitude. Yet in the end, few Americans were willing to go to war. The two countries settled the argument peacefully. They agreed that the 49th parallel would be the new boundary.

Negotiations with Mexico did not go quite so well. Polk had his mind set on purchasing California from Mexico. The Mexicans refused to take his offer seriously. Polk was not to be deterred. In the spring of 1846, he instigated a war, intent on gaining territory from Mexico.

Nearly two years later, the Mexican leaders were ready to bargain. The Treaty of Guadalupe Hidalgo ended the Mexican-American War. Mexico gave up almost half of its territory. The United States gained a clear title to Texas. In addition, all the territory to the west of Texas, including California, was now American soil.

▶ Oregon Fever

Once they arrived in the Willamette River valley, settlers wanted to attract more families to Oregon. To encourage others to come, they sent glowing reports back east. Pamphlets described the beauty of the land. The brochures often exaggerated and added amusing tales. One man, recruiting emigrants in 1843, went so far as to report that "out in Oregon the pigs are running about under the great acorn trees, round and fat, and already cooked, with knives and forks sticking in them so that you can cut off a slice whenever you are hungry."[4]

Settling the West was already a romantic notion in the minds of many Americans. Adventurers had written books describing their travels through the rugged American West. The public, eager for information about the frontier, gobbled them up. Men with a mind for business published guidebooks with information about moving west. With their stories of riches and opportunity, the emigrants succeeded in creating "Oregon Fever" back in the United States.

In 1850, Congress did its part to bring people to Oregon by passing the Donation Land Claim Act. It allowed a settler to claim, at no cost, 320 acres in Oregon's Willamette River valley. If he were married, his wife could claim an additional 320 acres. In those days, a woman's property belonged to her husband. This law was unusual, because it gave a married woman the right to own land. The only condition was that the settlers had to live on and farm the land for four years. This offer of free farmland was too good for some to pass up.

Chapter 3

SETTING OUT FOR THE FRONTIER

Although the Oregon Trail was a pathway through the wild, it was often far from lonely. On the trail's busiest years, the settlers reported seeing wagons stretched out across the land as far as the eye could see. Four hundred thousand people went west on the Oregon Trail between 1840 and 1880. The trip was over two thousand miles long. It took four to eight months to complete. What compelled the emigrants to leave behind their homes in the United States? Why did they go to settle on the Oregon frontier?

Manifest Destiny played a part. Yet people did not go west just for the good of their nation. All the emigrants believed they could make a better life for themselves. Some were following in the tradition of their parents and grandparents, who had emigrated west from Europe to America. Some were restless wanderers, searching for adventure. Some were criminals, hoping to escape the law. Others were drawn by the idea of free

A wagon train moseys along on the prairie following a portion of the Oregon Trail.

land. Some believed the stories that Oregon was a paradise. Some wanted to get away from society and live out in the wilderness.[1]

When gold was discovered in California in 1848, many schemers went west hoping to "get rich quick" panning for gold. Back in the United States, people were suffering through economic hard times. Americans had lost jobs and money in the Panic of 1837. Hundreds of banks failed. Factories closed and jobs became hard to find. Those lucky enough to have jobs found their wages cut nearly in half. Americans began to look hopefully to the West.

Outfitting a Prairie Schooner

To reach the frontier, most settlers first traveled to the gateway to the West: St. Louis, Missouri. The first leg of the settlers' journey was often a steamboat ride from St. Louis up the Missouri River to either the town of Independence or St. Joseph. The two Missouri towns competed to attract the emigrants. The steamboat ride shaved several days off the length of the trip west. Both Independence and St. Joseph were small, newly built frontier communities. In March, when most pioneers arrived, the towns bustled with energy and excitement. Merchants sold livestock, wagons, and food supplies. Each town boasted that it was a better point to "jump off" from. The competition

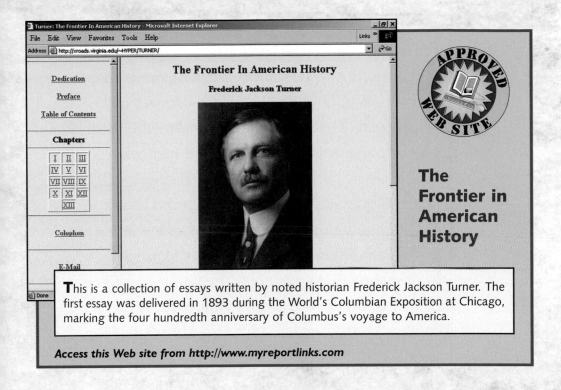

Turner: The Frontier In American History - Microsoft Internet Explorer

File   Edit   View   Favorites   Tools   Help   Links »

Address http://xroads.virginia.edu/~HYPER/TURNER/   Go

Dedication

Preface

Table of Contents

Chapters

I   II   III
IV   V   VI
VII VIII IX
X   XI XII
XIII

Coluphon

E-Mail

Done

The Frontier In American History

Frederick Jackson Turner

**The
Frontier in
American
History**

This is a collection of essays written by noted historian Frederick Jackson Turner. The first essay was delivered in 1893 during the World's Columbian Exposition at Chicago, marking the four hundredth anniversary of Columbus's voyage to America.

Access this Web site from http://www.myreportlinks.com

was fierce. There was good money in outfitting the emigrants.

Settlers often waited to purchase their supplies in Missouri. They wanted their food to be as fresh as possible when they began their trip. It was also best to buy livestock in Missouri. Animals accustomed to feeding on prairie grass fared better on the trail. The settlers waited in town until April, when the prairie grasses had turned green enough for their animals to eat. To the north, the town of Kanesville, Iowa, was the jumping-off point for most Mormon emigrants. Today the town of Kanesville is known as Council Bluffs.

People fondly called the covered wagons prairie schooners. A schooner is a sailboat. From a distance, the white canvas tarps of the wagons looked like sails gliding across a waving sea of prairie grass. The narrow wagon beds were made of wood. They were about four feet wide and ten to twelve feet long. The wagon boxes were fitted with hoops. Canvas stretched over the hoops to form a bonnet. The thick canvas or sailcloth bonnets were thoroughly soaked in linseed oil to keep out the worst of the weather. The bonnet could be cinched together with a pull string at the front and the back of the wagon. This also helped to keep out the dust.

The Undercarriage

Each wagon had two sets of wheels. The front wheels were sometimes smaller. This helped the wagons maneuver around turns. The wheels were made of a thin layer of iron covering a wooden frame. In the dry desert, the wooden spokes often shrunk. Then the iron rim would no longer fit onto the wooden frame. Settlers solved the problem by wedging small pieces of wood between the wheel frame and the rim. One of the worst problems the settlers could face was a broken axle. An axle is the shaft that the wheels turn on. Some settlers carried an extra axle under the wagon bed, but as it was heavy, it was often discarded along the way.

▲ Spokes and a wheel on the axle of an original Oregon Trail carriage. A broken axle was one of the worst problems that could happen to the emigrants.

The weighty wagons left deep wheel ruts in the ground. The ruts helped to mark the trail. Some of the wagon ruts are visible even today, nearly 150 years after the overland migration.

Dried Foods

What did the settlers eat along the way? A guide-book of the day warned people that they needed to bring plenty of provisions. They could not depend on eating wild game. Although bison and other animals were plentiful, the emigrants would be much too busy traveling to hunt for fresh meat every day.[2] They packed dried beans, flour, rice, cornmeal, sugar, salt, coffee, and tea in sturdy burlap bags. Along the way, they used saleratus for making biscuits and flapjacks. Saleratus, or sodium bicarbonate, is a leavening agent, commonly known as baking soda. Bacon was the meat of choice. If it were well preserved and stored, the heavily salted pork could last for months. A few bags of dried corn, apples, and peaches added some variety.

Cookware

There was not room for many pots and pans. Most families brought a few heavy, durable pans made of cast iron. The skillet, or frying pan, was essential for frying bacon and flapjacks. They cooked dried beans and biscuits in Dutch ovens. A Dutch oven is a cast iron pot with a cover. It could be set

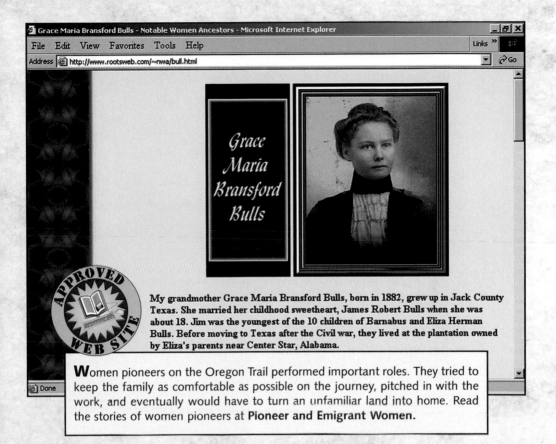

Grace Maria Bransford Bulls — Notable Women Ancestors - Microsoft Internet Explorer

File   Edit   View   Favorites   Tools   Help   Links »

Address   http://www.rootsweb.com/~nwa/bull.html   Go

Grace Maria Bransford Bulls

My grandmother Grace Maria Bransford Bulls, born in 1882, grew up in Jack County Texas. She married her childhood sweetheart, James Robert Bulls when she was about 18. Jim was the youngest of the 10 children of Barnabus and Eliza Herman Bulls. Before moving to Texas after the Civil war, they lived at the plantation owned by Eliza's parents near Center Star, Alabama.

Women pioneers on the Oregon Trail performed important roles. They tried to keep the family as comfortable as possible on the journey, pitched in with the work, and eventually would have to turn an unfamiliar land into home. Read the stories of women pioneers at **Pioneer and Emigrant Women.**

Done

directly in the coals of the fire. More coals were heaped around on all sides to cook the food faster. Some hopeful women packed their fine china dishes safely in the bottom of a trunk. If the china survived the trip to Oregon, it would decorate their homestead tables. On the trail, people used tin plates and cups. Unlike the delicate chinaware, tin was unbreakable.

Most wagon trains stopped for a few hours in the middle of the day for dinner. The emigrants called this hour-long break "nooning." The length of the respite often depended on the weather or the roughness of the terrain in a certain area. There was no time for campfires and a hot meal. They ate simple food such as cold beans cooked the night before and hardtack. Hardtack, also known as pilot bread, was a type of biscuit that had been cooked at a low heat for a long time. As a result, hardtack was very dry and not very flavorful. If it was kept dry, it could be stored for a long time.

Whenever they could, the emigrants supplemented their diet with fresh meat or fish. Wagon trains sent out small hunting parties. The men would set out on horses or on foot. If they were successful, they would tie the animal to the back of a horse and drag it back to camp. A large animal, such as a bison, deer, elk, antelope, or bighorn sheep, provided food for a crowd. The emigrants dried any leftover meat into jerky. They made smaller meals of prairie hens, rabbits, and grouse. Once they reached Idaho, the settlers might catch salmon or trout. When someone recognized an edible wild plant, the pioneers harvested as much as they could. Wild strawberries, chokecherries, and onions were treats.

Livestock

Many families took along a milking cow. Milking the cow each morning and evening was one more chore to fit into their busy day. The extra calories were worth it. If the evening milk sat overnight, in the morning a layer of cream rested on the milk's surface. The cream went into a butter churn. At home, women would make butter by turning the churn's hand crank until the cream thickened. On the trail, the bumping and rocking of the wagon did the work. At the end of the day there was butter to slather on the biscuits.

Some emigrants brought sheep, chickens, turkeys, hogs, or cattle along with them. It was a lot of extra work to drive a herd of animals along the trail. When traveling among strangers, the emigrants had to keep a constant eye out for

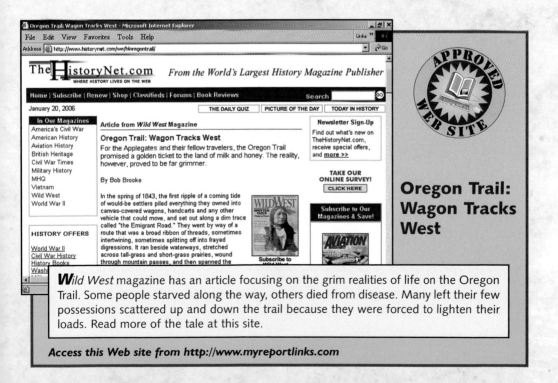

Wild West magazine has an article focusing on the grim realities of life on the Oregon Trail. Some people starved along the way, others died from disease. Many left their few possessions scattered up and down the trail because they were forced to lighten their loads. Read more of the tale at this site.

Access this Web site from http://www.myreportlinks.com

thieves. Hungry wolves on the prairie were another threat. If a settler could succeed in bringing farm animals west, there was money to be made. The settlers needed these animals for their new frontier farms.

▷ Working Together in a Wagon Train

It took some time for an emigrant family to buy all the provisions, animals, and equipment they would need. While they were shopping, they were also getting to know the other people who would be going west that year. Emigrants usually traveled in groups of at least twenty wagons. These wagon trains were called caravans. Cattle thieves were less likely to attack large parties of people.

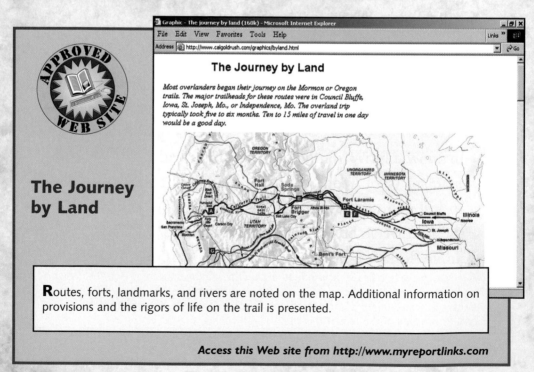

The Journey by Land

Routes, forts, landmarks, and rivers are noted on the map. Additional information on provisions and the rigors of life on the trail is presented.

Access this Web site from http://www.myreportlinks.com

There was another advantage to traveling in a caravan. A group of people had more skills than one family. A wagon train might include people with special talents, like a blacksmith, a carpenter, or a doctor. More people could tackle problems better and faster by working together. For instance, when they came to a large river, they could build rafts to ferry the wagons across.

Caravan Community

Caravans were sometimes made up of many families and groups of people from different parts of the country. Oftentimes the people in a wagon train knew each other. They were likely to be members of the same family, former community, or political group. It was important that the people traveling together could get along. They would need to be able to depend on one another through the many trials ahead. Once a caravan was formed, the men elected a captain, or leader. The captain chose where to camp each night and where to stop for the noontime meal. He organized the men to take turns standing sentry at night. The caravan, on occasion, also chose someone to "pilot" them through to Oregon. Many times the pilot was an experienced mountain man who had made the trip before. The pilot carried maps and chose the route. Usually he was paid a salary for his guidance and expertise. Everyone in the wagon train chipped in to pay the pilot. Most wagon trains, though, traveled without a designated pilot.

▶ Ox: the Pioneer's Best Friend

Oxen were the number-one choice of animal to pull the covered wagons. The giant oxen had incredible strength and a gentle, docile nature. On the downside, they moved at a slow, leisurely pace. Oxen pulled wagons at a rate of two miles per hour, and wagon trains traveled an average of twenty miles a day. Some pioneers used horses or mules instead. They were more expensive, but traveled much faster than oxen. Mules have a stubborn disposition. To the great frustration of their owners, they do not always follow orders.

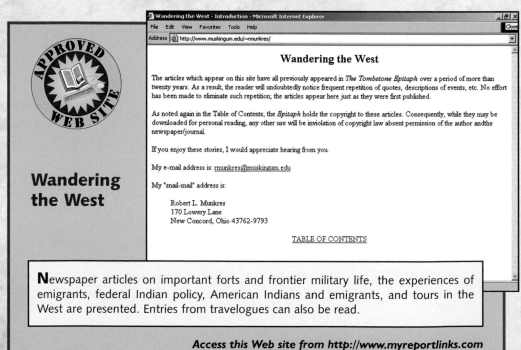

Wandering the West

Wandering the West - Introduction - Microsoft Internet Explorer

File   Edit   View   Favorites   Tools   Help

Address http://www.muskingum.edu/~rmunkres/

Wandering the West

The articles which appear on this site have all previously appeared in *The Tombstone Epitaph* over a period of more than twenty years. As a result, the reader will undoubtedly notice frequent repetition of quotes, descriptions of events, etc. No effort has been made to eliminate such repetition; the articles appear here just as they were first published.

As noted again in the Table of Contents, the *Epitaph* holds the copyright to these articles. Consequently, while they may be downloaded for personal reading, any other use will be inviolation of copyright law absent permission of the author andthe newspaper/journal.

If you enjoy these stories, I would appreciate hearing from you.

My e-mail address is: rmunkres@muskingum.edu

My "snail-mail" address is:

Robert L. Munkres
170 Lowery Lane
New Concord, Ohio 43762-9793

TABLE OF CONTENTS

Newspaper articles on important forts and frontier military life, the experiences of emigrants, federal Indian policy, American Indians and emigrants, and tours in the West are presented. Entries from travelogues can also be read.

Access this Web site from http://www.myreportlinks.com

With horses, there was the added risk of thieves. Laura Ingalls Wilder remembers her pioneer father saying, ". . . where there are deer there will be wolves, and where there are horses, there will be horse-thieves."[3] Most settlers (80 percent) chose to bring oxen. Oxen had the added benefit of only needing grass to browse on for food. Horses required the settlers to carry grain for feed.

Dangers to Oxen

Many overworked oxen died along the way. Others grew sick from drinking the alkaline water of the West. Alkaline water contains high levels of mineral salts. According to the diary of pioneer Abigail Jane Scott, the alkali ". . . looks about like ashes and has considerably the same taste only it is a great deal stronger."[4] An animal could even get sick from eating grass growing near alkaline water. The pioneers treated the animal by forcing a mixture of vinegar and animal fat down its throat. The fat coated the animal's stomach, while the acid of the vinegar counteracted the alkali. Ox bones were a common sight along the trail. The sun bleached the bones, making them clean and white. The settlers put the bones to good use. They wrote messages in pencil on the white surface. They set the bones where people following behind would notice them. They called bone writing the trailside telegraph.

North Platte

▲ *Fording rivers could be a stiff challenge for the emigrants. In this drawing, two covered wagons are being ferried across the Platte River in Wyoming. This sketch was done by Daniel A. Jenks.*

Ferries, Bridges, and River Fordings

Difficult river crossings were a nightmare for emigrants. In the early years of the Oregon Trail, there were no bridges spanning dangerous rivers. There were no ferries to float the wagons across on. Emigrants had to figure out creative ways to ford rivers. Many times, local American Indians would help them. They could drive the oxen across smaller streams without a problem. The wagon beds were purposely built high off the ground. If necessary, the beds could be raised even higher.[5]

The trouble came when wagon trains encountered deep rivers with strong currents. If an animal tired or panicked, the wagon could tip and break. Precious provisions would wash away. People, too, were at risk of drowning. At these times, the emigrants would unhook the animals from the wagons. They removed the wagon wheels and covered the wagon bed with buffalo hides. By rubbing tallow, or animal fat, and ashes onto the hides, they could waterproof their wagons. If there were plenty of trees, sometimes the emigrants camped on the river-bank for a few days. The men cut down trees and built rafts to carry the wagons across. The women used this time to catch up on laundry. They washed clothes in the river and hung them to dry on the bushes. The oxen, mules, cows, and horses often had to swim across deep rivers. The frightened animals often balked at the danger. They would only cross with much encouragement from the pioneers.

In later years, a few enterprising people had the foresight to build bridges and charge a toll to cross. Others operated ferries for a fee. They were offering a much-needed service, and people were willing to pay. The Mormons built a ferry to take themselves across the Platte River on their way to settle near the Great Salt Lake. Other emigrants asked to use the Mormon ferry service. The wide Platte River was especially difficult to cross. The river bottom was like quicksand. If you did not cross quickly, you risked getting sucked into the loose sand of the river bottom. Many preferred to pay for the ferry ride rather than risk their lives.

Chapter 4 ▶

OREGON FEVER—
"OREGON OR BUST!"

The emigrants confronted many nuisances on their trip west. Swarms of mosquitoes and sand fleas pestered them. The harsh sun beat down on their heads. To avoid sunburn, women wore cotton sunbonnets and the men donned wide-brimmed hats. On the prairies, thunderstorms developed quickly. Emigrants huddled inside their

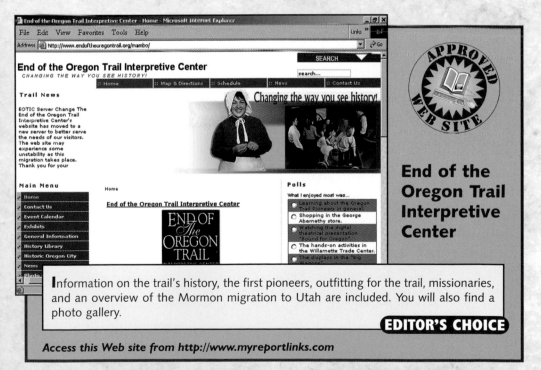

End of the Oregon Trail Interpretive Center

Information on the trail's history, the first pioneers, outfitting for the trail, missionaries, and an overview of the Mormon migration to Utah are included. You will also find a photo gallery.

EDITOR'S CHOICE

Access this Web site from http://www.myreportlinks.com

wagons to escape the high winds, torrents of rain, and hailstones. There was no way to stay completely dry in a driving rain, even inside the canvas-covered wagons. Once their clothing and equipment were thoroughly soaked, it might be days before it dried out again.

Daily Life on the Trail

The emigrants' nicest clothes stayed packed away in the wagon bed. They wore practical clothes day after day, for they rarely had a chance to wash. Despite the heat, men wore pants and long-sleeved shirts. Women wore long, heavy skirts and dresses. Thankfully, women's fashion turned a corner in the 1850s. Some women pioneers began wearing "bloomers," a kind of light, baggy pants puckered at the ankle and topped with a much shorter skirt.

The teams of oxen kicked up clouds of dust as they plodded across the dry grasslands. Dust got in the emigrants' hair, eyes, noses, and mouths. One emigrant wrote in her journal that "the dust today and for the last 100 miles or more has been verry (sic) annoying . . . allmost (sic) suffocating man and beast."[1] It was usually a boy's job to wipe the oxen's noses clean of dust with a damp rag. Whenever there was room, the wagons spread out across the prairie. Most people walked alongside rather than suffer a jolting, bumpy ride in a full wagon. Young children hopped up for a ride when they grew tired of walking.

The wagons were ideal for traveling across the flat prairie. Climbing hills slowed the caravans down considerably. When the wagons reached a steep incline, more animals than usual were needed to pull a wagon to the top. The wagon train would stop at the foot of the steep hill. The settlers would take turns hitching additional oxen to their wagons. There was always the possibility that a wagon would tip over, spilling its contents. On the way down, there was the risk that the wagon could gain momentum and overtake the slow-moving oxen. Sometimes the pioneers dragged a felled tree behind. The additional weight slowed the wagon down. Another trick was to wrap a rope from the wagon around a tree. Then they would slowly let out the rope, easing the wagon down the hill.

▶ Circle Up!

At the end of the day, the tired, dusty pioneers looked for a campsite to call home for the night. They needed a spot that had water within carrying distance and plenty of grass for the animals to eat. They pulled their wagons into a tight circle. The men set the animals free on the prairies to graze on the best grass they could find. In the evening, the animals were penned up inside the wagon

These trail seekers are circling up the wagons to make camp. This is near Bayard, Nebraska.

circle. Oxen and cows were unlikely to wander too far. Horses and mules, however, would roam far from camp if they were allowed. Using rope and a stake, the settlers tethered them to the ground. The wagon corral also protected the livestock from thieves. People feared American Indians would steal their animals.

The emigrants built campfires and prepared the evening meal on the outside of the circle. The children gathered fuel for the fire. When they could not find dead wood, they collected buffalo chips. The dried animal dung burned clean, without an odor. Women prepared dinners of beans and bacon. They went for water to cook and clean with. After walking all day, everyone was thirsty. Often the water tasted bad. To make it palatable, they boiled it and made coffee or tea. Some days, successful hunters would contribute fresh game to roast over the fires. Friendly American Indian tribes gave food to the emigrants, especially in the early years of the trail. In later years, misunderstandings and resentments between the emigrants and the American Indians grew so bad that they sometimes became lethal.

▶ Entertainment

Although they must have been bone tired, the pioneers did not go without entertainment. After dinner, people relaxed and chatted with their neighbors. On some nights, musical instruments appeared from their hiding spots inside the wagons. Around the glowing campfires, people played dancing tunes on harmonicas and fiddles. The overlanders sang along to the day's popular songs. Still, the next day would be another long one. Before the moon grew too high in the sky, everyone crawled into a tent or his or her wagon for the night. Men took turns standing sentry, watching over the safety of the camp and the animals. Before sunrise, the last sentry gave the wake-up call. His shout turned the camp into a hive of action. People often slept in their clothes, so they had one less chore to do in the morning. The animals were

"Emigrants Crossing the Plains" is a famous engraving by Felix Darley and Henry Bryan Hall. It is a dramatic depiction of what life was like on the Oregon Trail.

gathered and hitched to the wagons. The emigrants enjoyed a quick breakfast of flapjacks, coffee, and bacon. Everything was stuffed back into its spot on the wagon. Everyone had to be ready to go when the call came at six o'clock in the morning to hit the trail.

Abandoned Pianos on the Prairie

Pioneers often started out the journey with as much as they could carry. They packed everything they imagined they might need to make a new home on the frontier. They brought dining tables, chairs, bureaus, trunks of fine clothes, china dishes, and even an occasional piano. It took an average of three oxen to pull each heavy wagon. Along the way, pioneers quickly learned the truth about the rigors of the trail. Heavy wagons slowed the oxen down. Pulling too heavy a load could injure or even kill an animal. To lighten their loads, settlers abandoned many unnecessary items. Heirloom furniture and woodstoves littered the trailside.

Death on the Trail

Going west was a risky endeavor. One historian estimates that ten thousand people died along the way.[2] Others claim that twenty-five to thirty thousand deaths is a more accurate figure.[3] Both true reports and false rumors of Indian attacks spread like wildfire along the trail. Many settlers so

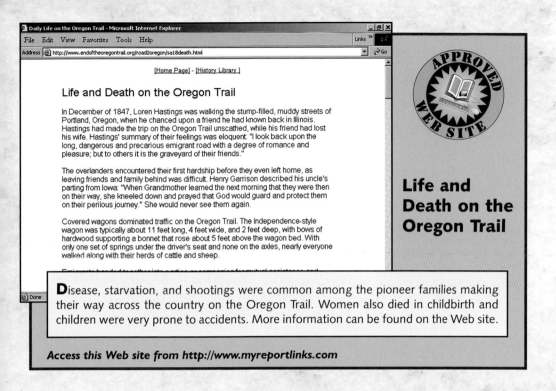

Life and Death on the Oregon Trail

Daily Life on the Oregon Trail - Microsoft Internet Explorer

File   Edit   View   Favorites   Tools   Help   Links »

Address   http://www.endoftheoregontrail.org/road2oregon/sa18death.html   Go

[Home Page] - [History Library]

Life and Death on the Oregon Trail

In December of 1847, Loren Hastings was walking the stump-filled, muddy streets of Portland, Oregon, when he chanced upon a friend he had known back in Illinois. Hastings had made the trip on the Oregon Trail unscathed, while his friend had lost his wife. Hastings' summary of their feelings was eloquent: "I look back upon the long, dangerous and precarious emigrant road with a degree of romance and pleasure; but to others it is the graveyard of their friends."

The overlanders encountered their first hardship before they even left home, as leaving friends and family behind was difficult. Henry Garrison described his uncle's parting from Iowa: "When Grandmother learned the next morning that they were then on their way, she kneeled down and prayed that God would guard and protect them on their perilous journey." She would never see them again.

Covered wagons dominated traffic on the Oregon Trail. The Independence-style wagon was typically about 11 feet long, 4 feet wide, and 2 feet deep, with bows of hardwood supporting a bonnet that rose about 5 feet above the wagon bed. With only one set of springs under the driver's seat and none on the axles, nearly everyone walked along with their herds of cattle and sheep.

Done

Disease, starvation, and shootings were common among the pioneer families making their way across the country on the Oregon Trail. Women also died in childbirth and children were very prone to accidents. More information can be found on the Web site.

Access this Web site from http://www.myreportlinks.com

feared Indians that they carried their firearms at all times. Indeed, some settlers died when their guns went off by accident.

Although American Indians and settlers occasionally had deadly encounters, the risk of Indian attack was greatly exaggerated. In reality, the pioneers were more likely to drown as they were to be killed by an American Indian. The more dangerous threat was disease. Disease accounted for nine out of ten deaths along the trail. The pioneers had to contend with common diseases of the nineteenth century like measles, mumps, typhoid, and malaria. Thanks to modern medicine, these diseases are no longer a problem in the United

States. Dysentery was probably the most common ailment of the pioneers. Eating spoiled food or drinking contaminated water often caused it. Most of the settlers suffered the painful cramps, diarrhea, and vomiting of dysentery at one time or another.

▶ Cholera

The most frightening disease of all was cholera. Cholera is caused by bacteria that infect the intestines. If it went untreated, cholera could kill a perfectly healthy person within a matter of a few hours. Between 1848 and 1855, an epidemic of Asian cholera swept across America. It reached Missouri in 1849. The disease, which is spread when people drink or use contaminated water, spread rapidly in the poor hygienic conditions on the trail. Unfortunately, people did not yet know what caused cholera. They could only watch helplessly as it infected their wagon parties.

When sickness struck, it could be hard to find a doctor. Lucky caravans had a doctor traveling with them. He could help people recover and prescribe medicine to ease their pain. Some doctors rode up and down the trail, helping people where they could. Otherwise, a sick person had to wait to reach a trading post to see a doctor. Emigrants packed their own medicine kits in case of emergency. Their kits often included laudanum, camphor, castor oil, whiskey, and dried herbs. They carried citric acid to prevent scurvy. Scurvy is a deficiency of vitamin C, a vitamin found in the fresh fruits and vegetables that their diets sorely lacked.

During the worst years of the cholera epidemic, emigrants often noted in their journals how many graves they passed each day. Not wanting to fall behind, the hurried settlers sometimes did a poor job burying the bodies. People passing in later wagons were horrified to see that coyotes and wolves had dug up the remains of shallow graves. American Indians occasionally scavenged clothing from graves. They did not know the clothes were contaminated with deadly diseases. To ensure the graves would be undisturbed, the emigrants

▲ Historians estimate that anywhere between ten thousand and thirty thousand people died along the Oregon Trail. These victims were remembered with monuments, but most were buried in unmarked graves.

learned to hide them. They buried the dead right in the middle of the trail. The stomping of feet and the turning of the wagon wheels removed all signs of the recently dug graves. That is why, though anywhere from ten thousand to thirty thousand people may have died, very few marked graves are visible along the historic trail.

Are We There Yet?

As everyone who has been on a long car trip understands, it is helpful to know how far you have gone and how much longer you still need to travel. The pioneers eagerly looked for landmarks along the way. The landmarks reassured them that they were making good time and traveling on the right path. The Oregon Trail followed the wide Platte River for hundreds of miles through Nebraska and Wyoming. The shallow Platte was difficult to boat on, dotted as it was with mudflats. The river was constantly changing course. Many fallen trees lay submerged under the murky water.

After weeks of travel along the flat grasslands, the emigrants were overjoyed to see sandstone Courthouse Rock and Jail Rock towering above the Nebraska prairie. Another remarkable feature on the prairie was a natural rock tower called Chimney Rock. At 500 feet tall, it looms over the surrounding flat land. The emigrants could see the rock formation for days before they reached it.

Pioneer Abigail Jane Scott wrote in her diary, "After traveling a while in the afternoon we came in sight of the long heard of and renowned Chimney Rock; It at first looked as if it were a spire pointing towards Heaven's blue dome but as we came nearer to it the spire seemed to enlarge and bear rather more the appearance of a chimney extending high above a dome shaped building."[4]

Emigrants tried to reach Independence Rock, in present-day Wyoming by the nation's birthday,

▲ Chimney Rock was one of the most well-liked and majestic landmarks along the Oregon Trail. It is located in Bayard, Nebraska.

July 4. The impressive granite boulder is 100 feet high, 2,000 feet long, and 700 feet wide. The rock served as a register—a kind of guest book of the trail. The settlers clambered up the rock, armed with a knife to carve their names and the date. Some wrote their names with homemade paint consisting of grease and gunpowder. They also read through the names of people, hoping to recognize someone they might know from home.

Forts and Other Landmarks

Forts were landmarks that had the extra benefit of providing a safe place to rest. There the pioneers could mail letters home. They could visit the fort's sutler, or merchant, to stock up on supplies. They could trade worn-out animals for fresh ones. There was a blacksmith to shoe horses and oxen. A doctor tended to the sick. Many of the forts had originally served the fur trade. When Americans began emigrating to the West, they argued that the United States government had a duty to protect the Oregon Trail from hostile American Indians. In 1848, the United States built Fort Kearny, on the Platte River. Soon, soldiers manned this and other forts along the trail. American Indians also used the forts as a place to trade. They set up tepee villages outside the fort walls.

At the curious Ice Slough, the thirsty pioneers were amazed to find ice in the middle of the hot desert. The refreshing ice was kept cool by the peat moss growing in a bog there.

The Oregon Trail cut through the Rocky Mountains at the South Pass in present-day Wyoming. The South Pass was a 30-mile-wide prairie. At the South Pass, the emigrants crossed over the Continental Divide. On one side of the divide, rivers flow east to the Mississippi River. On the other, the water drains to the west. The Continental Divide was perhaps the landmark the emigrants celebrated most. Though many miles of their journey remained ahead of them, they had

The South Pass was the easiest way for overland travelers to cut through the Rocky Mountains. Emigrants were happy to reach it because it meant they were getting close to the end, but the remaining road ahead was very challenging. **Oregon National Historic Trail** Web site is a fine place to learn about the South Pass and other aspects of the trail. **EDITOR'S CHOICE**

finally reached Oregon Country. Now they looked forward to seeing the infamous springs they had heard about. Steamboat Springs in Idaho gave off a loud whistle that reminded the emigrants of the steamboats back home. The bubbling Soda Springs had refreshing, carbonated water. Some emigrants added sugar and vinegar to make a drink that reminded them of soda.[5]

The Chinook nation lived along the Columbia River near the town of The Dalles and carved this face of a woman into the rock. It is named Tsagiglalal or "She Who Watches." American Indians often helped emigrants ford the river at this point.

In Idaho, after Fort Hall, the trail branched in two directions. One fork led on to the Willamette River valley in Oregon, while the other set off toward San Francisco, California. Here the wagon trains split, and the pioneers said good-bye to their companions as they went their separate ways. Emigrants headed to Oregon continued overland to The Dalles. In The Dalles, there is a series of rapids on the Columbia River called the Long Narrows and Short Narrows. This is where the dangerous final leg of the trip began. The settlers, often led by American Indian pilots, rafted their belongings down the Columbia River. In several spots the river runs so rapidly that they carried their belongings along the bank. It was often late in the autumn when the emigrants finally reached their destination. They were exhausted from their journey. Many had run out of food and money. There was a mad race to build shelter and gather supplies before the winter rains came. In the spirit of the frontier, people pitched in to help one another. The following spring, they began the work of tilling the soil and planting food crops.

▶ Seeing the Elephant

Not all who set out for Oregon completed the trip. Some decided the rough conditions of the trail were not for them. Some simply grew homesick for civilization. Most of the "go backs," as they were called, returned to the States because they

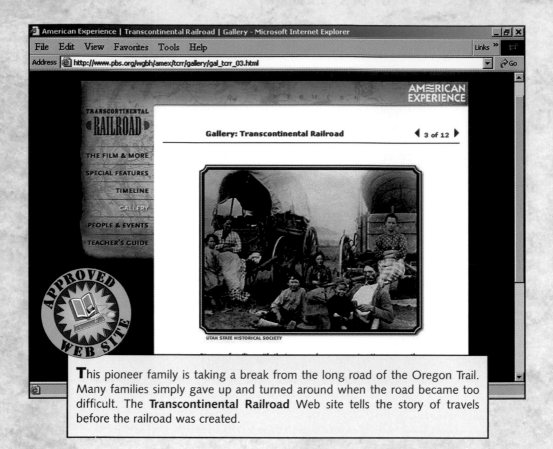

American Experience | Transcontinental Railroad | Gallery - Microsoft Internet Explorer

File   Edit   View   Favorites   Tools   Help   Links »

Address http://www.pbs.org/wgbh/amex/tcrr/gallery/gal_tcrr_03.html   Go

AMERICAN
EXPERIENCE

TRANSCONTINENTAL
RAILROAD

THE FILM & MORE
SPECIAL FEATURES
TIMELINE
GALLERY
PEOPLE & EVENTS
TEACHER'S GUIDE

Gallery: Transcontinental Railroad   ◀ 3 of 12 ▶

UTAH STATE HISTORICAL SOCIETY

This pioneer family is taking a break from the long road of the Oregon Trail. Many families simply gave up and turned around when the road became too difficult. The **Transcontinental Railroad** Web site tells the story of travels before the railroad was created.

found they could not go on. Perhaps they lost their wagon and supplies in a river crossing. Maybe their oxen died and could not be replaced. Some families were forced to turn around because of the death of a family member. When folks gave up and returned home, the emigrants said they had "seen the elephant." This odd phrase meant they had seen enough and were ready to head home. People headed against the flow of foot traffic found they were very popular. Everyone wanted to talk with them to find out what lay in store ahead.

Chapter 5

FAMOUS PEOPLE OF THE OREGON TRAIL

It required courage to settle in the remote West. Even the most typical pioneer undertook a great adventure in traveling on the Oregon Trail. Among the pioneers there were many heroic figures. Yet there are some names that are heard over and over again. These are people who were not afraid to be the first to try something new. They were daring trailblazers, sometimes quite literally. Some grew rich through a mixture of hard work and good fortune. Others are famous because their actions helped other people.

▶ Astor Opens Oregon to American Trade

John Jacob Astor was just another young man with big dreams when he emigrated from Germany. He arrived in New York City with very little. His marriage brought him connections to the city's shipping industry. By 1809, the hardworking Astor had built an empire for himself. He traveled to Montreal each fall to trade for furs with American Indians. Astor then shipped the furs to Europe and China where they fetched an exorbitant price.

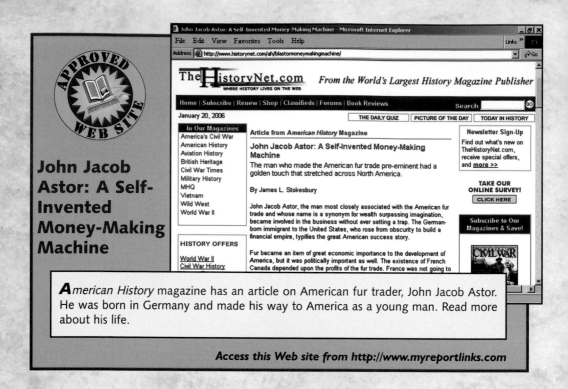

File   Edit   View   Favorites   Tools   Help   Links »

Address http://www.historynet.com/ah/blastormoneymakingmachine/   Go

The HistoryNet.com   *From the World's Largest History Magazine Publisher*
WHERE HISTORY LIVES ON THE WEB

Home | Subscribe | Renew | Shop | Classifieds | Forums | Book Reviews   Search   GO

January 20, 2006   THE DAILY QUIZ   PICTURE OF THE DAY   TODAY IN HISTORY

In Our Magazines
America's Civil War   Article from *American History* Magazine
American History
Aviation History   **John Jacob Astor: A Self-Invented Money-Making**
British Heritage   **Machine**
Civil War Times   The man who made the American fur trade pre-eminent had a
Military History   golden touch that stretched across North America.
MHQ
Vietnam   By James L. Stokesbury
Wild West
World War II   John Jacob Astor, the man most closely associated with the American fur
                          trade and whose name is a synonym for wealth surpassing imagination,
                          became involved in the business without ever setting a trap. The German-
HISTORY OFFERS   born immigrant to the United States, who rose from obscurity to build a
                          financial empire, typifies the great American success story.
World War II
Civil War History   Fur became an item of great economic importance to the development of
                          America, but it was politically important as well. The existence of French
                          Canada depended upon the profits of the fur trade. France was not going to

Newsletter Sign-Up
Find out what's new on
TheHistoryNet.com,
receive special offers,
and **more >>**

**TAKE OUR
ONLINE SURVEY!**
CLICK HERE

Subscribe to Our
Magazines & Save!

John Jacob Astor: A Self-Invented Money-Making Machine

American History magazine has an article on American fur trader, John Jacob Astor.
He was born in Germany and made his way to America as a young man. Read more
about his life.

Access this Web site from http://www.myreportlinks.com

Ever a shrewd businessman, Astor expanded his
fur business. He knew the Hudson's Bay Company
had already begun trading with the American
Indians of the Pacific Northwest. Astor established
the Pacific Fur Company in 1810. Astor dreamed
of building trading posts throughout the Louisiana
Territory and on to Oregon. He succeeded in
building one fort, Astoria, on the Columbia River.
Astor's efforts helped to open up Oregon for further American settlement and trade. As the fur
trade grew less profitable, he transferred his
money into New York real estate. Astor owned so
many buildings that he gained the nickname

"Landlord of New York." Upon his death in 1838, his estate was valued at $30 million.

Mountain Man Jim Bridger

Jim Bridger was a true mountain man. As a fur trapper he learned about the Rocky Mountain region and the American Indians who lived there. When the fur trade slowed, Bridger turned his knowledge toward helping the emigrants. He knew they would need services, advice, and supplies. In 1843, Bridger and his friend and fellow mountain man, Louis Vasquez, built a trading post on a branch of the Green River of southwest Wyoming. Fort Bridger was the first trail fort built

This is an image of the stables at Fort Bridger. This fort was named after Jim Bridger, a famous fur trapper and mountain man.

specifically to meet the needs of the overland emigrants. The fort also served as a trading post for the area's American Indians. Bridger was well known for his friendly ties with American Indian tribes. In fact, these ties may have got him into trouble with the Mormon leader, Brigham Young. As the story goes, the Mormons were at war with the Ute Indians. Young declared it illegal to trade with American Indians. Bridger did not comply, and a band of Mormons set out for Fort Bridger to arrest the mountain man. They never captured him, for Bridger was tipped off that they were coming for him. The Mormons did manage to put an end to Fort Bridger. In 1855, Bridger and Vasquez sold the fort to the Mormons for eight thousand dollars.[1]

Stuart Finds the South Pass

With few prospects for work in his native Scottish highlands, the young Robert Stuart came to Montreal to work in the fur trade. He got his lucky break when he joined Astor's Pacific Fur Company as a junior partner. Stuart sailed to the Pacific Northwest where he helped to build Astoria. In June 1812, Stuart set off by canoe up the Columbia River. He had drawn the task of trekking overland to the United States. He was carrying letters for Astor, who had not heard from the fort in nearly a year.[2] Instead of following Lewis and

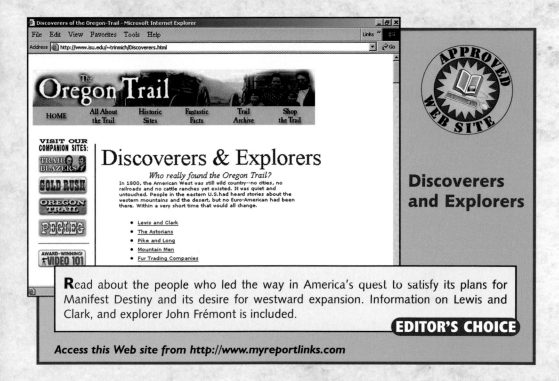

Access this Web site from http://www.myreportlinks.com

Clark's trail, Stuart's party veered south. They found themselves trying to cross the snowy Rocky Mountains in October. The mountains seemed insurmountable. Taking the advice of Shoshone Indians, Stuart followed the Wind River.[3] It led his party to a low gap through the mountains. The climb was so gradual that it was hard to believe they had crossed the immense mountain range. This gap came to be known as the South Pass. Although Stuart told Astor about the pass, few others knew about it until 1843. In that year, the United States government sent explorer John C. Frémont to map routes to the West. Both the Oregon Trail and the Mormon Trail to Great Salt

Lake used the South Pass. Without it, wagons would never have crossed the Rockies.

Sublette: Trail Forerunner

William Sublette was a fur trader. Like John Jacob Astor, he made his living buying and selling furs. Sublette worked out of St. Louis, Missouri. He employed such famous mountain men as Joseph Meek to trap beaver in the Rockies. Sublette would ride out to meet the mountain men each year. The mountaineers would swap beaver pelts in exchange for supplies. In 1830, Sublette was on his way to the annual rendezvous. He brought ten wagons full of supplies to their meeting point on the Wind River in present-day Wyoming. In doing so, Sublette became the first man to take wagons across the Continental Divide. Sublette's path later became part of the Oregon Trail. He also built Fort Laramie in present-day Wyoming. Many emigrants later used this fur trading post.

Missionaries Bring Light to the Wilderness

Some of the earliest people to travel to Oregon were Christian missionaries. The Methodists chose the Reverend Jason Lee to represent them in Oregon. Reverend Lee and a small group of missionaries traveled to the Willamette Valley with fur traders in 1834. Upon his arrival, Lee decided that a small village of retired French

Father Pierre-Jean de Smet was a Catholic missionary that served the American Indians of the Oregon Country. He was known for keeping peace between the tribes and the white government.

Canadian fur trappers and their American Indian wives was the best place for his assistance. The village raised crops for nearby Fort Vancouver, Hudson's Bay Company's trading center in the Pacific Northwest. Lee and his missionaries planted crops, built houses, and began a school. His achievements were inspirational for other missionaries. The Whitmans and the Spaldings arrived in 1836. They worked among the Cayuse and Nez Percé. Catholic Father Pierre-Jean de Smet came to Oregon in 1840. Father de Smet gained the respect of many American Indians. He often helped mediate treaties between the government and the tribes.

▶ Walkers: Oregon's First True Emigrants

In 1840, Joel Walker, his wife, Mary, their four children, and Mary's sister, Martha Young, became the first emigrants to arrive in Oregon. They were not the first people—that honor would go to the American Indians. Nor were they the first non-Indians to call it home. Fur trappers, traders, and missionaries had set up shop there decades earlier. The Walker family was simply the first to travel to Oregon with the sole purpose of settling there. As the trail was not yet well worn and easy to follow, the Walkers needed some help finding the way. They traveled with a party of fur traders and missionaries to Fort Hall. There the family left its wagons, believing the way ahead was too rough.[4]

The Bidwell-Bartleson company has the distinction of being the first overland emigrant wagon train. They set off from Missouri, headed for California in 1841. Along the way some of the emigrants decided to settle in Oregon.

▶ Oregon's Long Arm of the Law

Born in Virginia in 1804, Joseph Meek was one of the early fur trappers of the American West. After the collapse of the fur trade, he made a name for himself as a guide. In 1840, Meek led a group of missionaries to the Fort Hall trading post. He and his friend Robert Newell decided to continue on all the way to Oregon. They took the missionaries' discarded wagons for transportation. With no blazed wagon trail, they fought their way through the heavy sagebrush. The trip was extremely difficult, yet they made it. As a reward, the men would go down in history as the first people to bring wagons all the way to Oregon. The pair rested at the Whitman's mission before heading on to settle in the Willamette Valley.

It was Meek who brought the news of the Whitman Massacre to the United States. The Whitmans had been his good friends. Meek's ten-year-old daughter, Helen, was staying with the Whitmans at the time of the massacre. She

The Cayuse Indians were the tribe involved in the Whitman Massacre after the relationship between themselves and the white missionaries turned sour. This is an image of Chief Umapine of the Cayuse taken around 1913.

became ill and died soon after the Whitman's were killed. Angry and grieving, Meek traveled in haste back east on the Oregon Trail. It was a cold, snowy trip, leaving as he did in the late winter. Meek represented the Oregon settlers who hoped to gain President Polk's support in punishing the Cayuse. The president appointed Meek to be the first United States Marshal of the new Oregon Territory in 1849. Meek, the president's cousin, carried out the sentence of the Oregon jury who condemned the Cayuse murderers.

▶ Young Leads Mormons to Freedom

An American named Joseph Smith founded the Church of Jesus Christ of Latter-day Saints in 1830. Followers of Smith's church are called Mormons. In the 1830s and 1840s, the Mormons faced persecution from their neighbors. The Mormons were different from most Americans because they lived and worked together in a religious community. Some church members practiced polygamy, or marrying more than one wife. Other Americans found these practices intolerable and harassed the Mormons. To defend themselves, the Mormons developed their own militia. Smith and his group moved around the Midwest, from Ohio to Missouri and on to Illinois. In 1844, an angry, anti-Mormon mob murdered Smith.

A lively man named Brigham Young stepped forward as the church's new leader. Brigham Young took a group of Mormon pioneers west on the Oregon Trail in 1846. Like most emigrants, they brought livestock and drove covered wagons. While typical wagon trains were made up of young families, the Mormons brought their entire community west. Distrustful of the other emigrants, the Mormons kept to themselves. They traveled along the opposite bank of the Platte River. The Mormon Trail veered from the Oregon Trail into the Great Salt Lake valley. The isolated semidesert

Learn about Joseph Smith from this site titled **American Prophet: The Story of Joseph Smith.** Biographical information, his teachings and prophecies, along with the history of the Church of Jesus Christ of Latter-day Saints, is included.

near the Great Salt Lake became a homeland for the Latter-day Saints.

The industrious Mormons worked together to grow successful crops in the arid land. Thousands of Mormons from the United States and Europe joined Brigham Young in Utah. Later groups of Mormon emigrants arrived several weeks faster by pushing their own handcarts. In the new land, Mormons were free to practice their religion. However, the issue of polygamy, which has been illegal in the United States since 1862, kept Utah from gaining statehood until 1896. Today the Church of Jesus Christ of Latter-day Saints continues to thrive in the state of Utah.

Luelling: Fruit Grower With Foresight

Henderson Luelling was a Quaker from Iowa who decided to make a new start in the Oregon Country. Along with his personal possessions, Luelling brought extra wagons packed with young fruit trees, grapevines, and raspberry bushes. Luelling tended the plants carefully. He brought them safely across rivers and through bad weather. His orchards did well in the climate of Oregon. His apples, pears, peaches, plums, and cherries were in high demand. Unlike many unlucky gold miners, Luelling became a frontier millionaire.

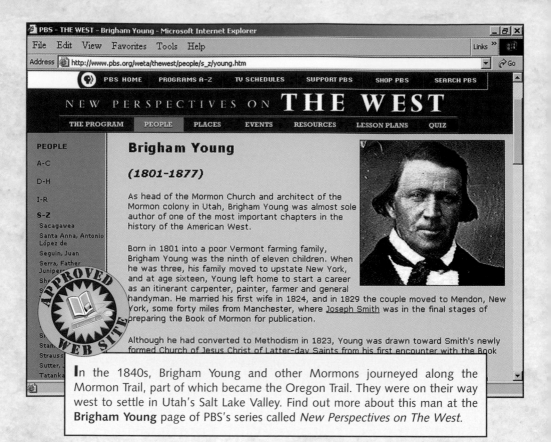

In the 1840s, Brigham Young and other Mormons journeyed along the Mormon Trail, part of which became the Oregon Trail. They were on their way west to settle in Utah's Salt Lake Valley. Find out more about this man at the **Brigham Young** page of PBS's series called *New Perspectives on The West*.

▶ Barlow and the Toll Road

Until 1846, the only route to Oregon's Willamette Valley included a raft trip down the Columbia River. The trail came to an abrupt end when it reached The Dalles on the Columbia River. Here the banks of the river turned to steep, impassable cliffs. The emigrants had to wait for a pilot to ferry them downstream. Those who could not afford a guide built their own rafts. It was a very dangerous journey through the rapid waters of the Columbia. People often drowned. Sometimes the

US BARLOW ROAD FS

FIRST ROAD BUILT OVER CASCADE RANGE
IN 1845 - 1846 BY
SAMUEL K. BARLOW (1792-1867)
AN OREGON PIONEER FROM KENTUCKY

▲ This sign marks the Barlow Road, a toll road built by Samuel Barlow to get settlers across the Cascade Mountains.

tired settlers had to wait a long time for a river guide to take them downriver. When Samuel Barlow arrived at The Dalles in 1845, he was dismayed by the dangerous river trip. He swore there must be a better way. The next year, Barlow completed a rough overland route from The Dalles to the Willamette Valley. He put a gate at either end and charged a toll to those who used the road. The fee was five dollars, a very steep price in those days. Barlow's road led through some dense forest. Settlers complained it contained some of the steepest hills of the entire trip. Still, many were thankful to continue overland rather than risk drowning.

▶ Parkman's *Oregon Trail*

Perhaps the most famous story of the Oregon Trail is not about the pioneers at all. Francis Parkman traveled through the West in 1846. His observations from that trip became the basis for his classic book of adventure, *The Oregon Trail*. Parkman, a wealthy New Englander, received his education at Harvard. Despite the name of his book, Parkman had little to say about the emigrants. Instead, his book is a highly entertaining story of his travels. Parkman described the beautiful American West in great detail. He wrote, in particular, about the American Indians he encountered. His book captures a place and time that was changing rapidly.

Author Francis Parkman

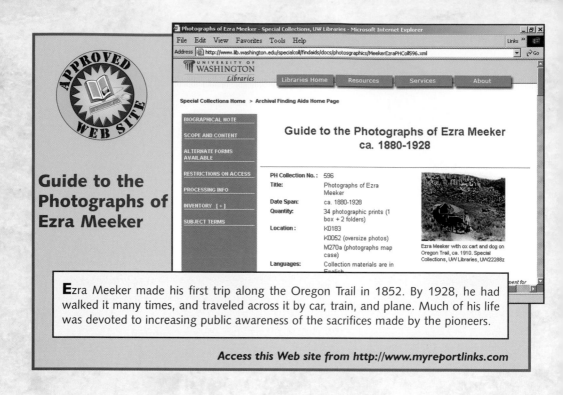

Ezra Meeker made his first trip along the Oregon Trail in 1852. By 1928, he had walked it many times, and traveled across it by car, train, and plane. Much of his life was devoted to increasing public awareness of the sacrifices made by the pioneers.

Access this Web site from http://www.myreportlinks.com

▶ Meeker Marks the Oregon Trail

Ezra Meeker traveled overland in 1852 as a young man. He settled near Puyallup, Washington. As Meeker grew older, he realized the Oregon Trail was disappearing. At age seventy-six, he decided to bring the trail back into the minds of the American people. In a covered wagon pulled by oxen, Meeker followed the old trail back east. It had not been used in years. Along the way, he stopped to talk with others who remembered the days of the great western emigration. He gave speeches about the history of the trail. Meeker encouraged towns to preserve the historic trail.

▲ *Ezra Meeker worked to preserve the Oregon Trail.*

When Meeker arrived in the East, he received permission to drive his wagon through the streets of New York City. He went to Washington, D.C., where he met with President Theodore Roosevelt. Meeker dedicated the remainder of his life to making sure the Oregon Trail would not be forgotten.

IMPACT OF THE OREGON TRAIL

The overland journey of the American settlers was one of the greatest migrations in world history. Has there been another time when so many people traveled so far through such wilderness? The story of the Oregon Trail is the story of how the United States grew to be what it is today. Due to the pioneers, American democracy spread across the continent. The arrival of thousands of American settlers tipped the scales in favor of American ownership of Oregon. In 1846, the British gave up their claim to the Columbia and the lush Willamette Valley. By 1859, Oregon had become the thirty-third state of the Union.

▷ The Iron Horse

With so many people migrating west, it was just a matter of time before they discovered a faster means of travel. In the 1850s, horse-drawn stage-coaches carried mail and passengers from Missouri to California. The trip, for those who had the money, could be made in less than a month. In

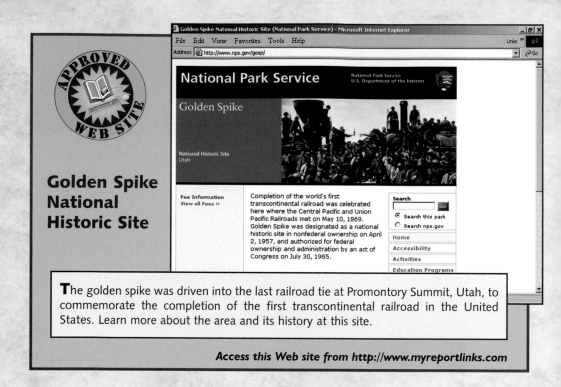

Golden Spike National Historic Site

National Park Service

National Park Service
U.S. Department of the Interior

Golden Spike

National Historic Site
Utah

Fee Information
View all Fees »

Completion of the world's first transcontinental railroad was celebrated here where the Central Pacific and Union Pacific Railroads met on May 10, 1869. Golden Spike was designated as a national historic site in nonfederal ownership on April 2, 1957, and authorized for federal ownership and administration by an act of Congress on July 30, 1965.

Search

Go

- Search this park
- Search nps.gov

Home

Accessibility

Activities

Education Programs

The golden spike was driven into the last railroad tie at Promontory Summit, Utah, to commemorate the completion of the first transcontinental railroad in the United States. Learn more about the area and its history at this site.

Access this Web site from http://www.myreportlinks.com

1862, Congress passed the Pacific Railroad Bill. The bill loaned government money to two companies for the purpose of building a railroad. The two companies were the Union Pacific and the Central Pacific. The completed railway would carry people and freight from the Midwest to the Pacific Coast. At first, there was debate over where the first overland train should go: to the north, south, or through the middle of the country. In the end, the route was built along the Platte River. It was the same wide, muddy river followed by the Oregon Trail. Irish and Chinese laborers toiled under dangerous conditions to clear land and lay train tracks. The Transcontinental Railroad was completed in 1869. The new railway service would make the trip from Nebraska to California in just six days. Fewer people chose to take months to go west in covered wagons. Large families and poor people still used the Oregon Trail, as it was the cheaper route. By the twentieth century, the westward migration of the pioneers and their prairie schooners was a thing of the past.

▶ The Other Story

The Oregon Trail also has another story to tell— the story of how American Indians lost their land. Today the American Indian population is growing. These people are proud of their American Indian ancestry. There is renewed interest in traditional

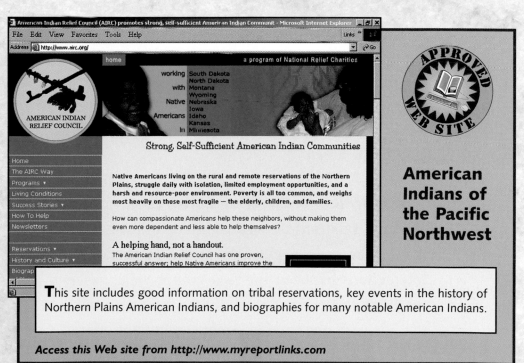

This site includes good information on tribal reservations, key events in the history of Northern Plains American Indians, and biographies for many notable American Indians.

Access this Web site from http://www.myreportlinks.com

American Indian cultures. But at the end of the nineteenth century, the fate of the tribes looked extremely bleak. Disease, starvation, and battle had killed off their people. Those that remained lost their land to the settlers. The United States government set aside land for the displaced American Indians. Often these reservations were near or part of their original homeland. Sometimes the reservations were far away, or on poor land that no one wanted. American Indians were given a choice: move onto a reservation or assimilate into American society. The government established boarding schools for the reservations' children. At school, the children were not allowed to talk to each other in their native language. They learned to speak and read English. As a result, many forgot their native tongues. They were taught that the American Indian way of life was bad. Instead of learning from their parents, they learned how to live like their teachers: white, Christian Americans.

▶ The Frontier: A Clash of Cultures

How did relations between settlers and American Indians eventually grow so grim? At first, most interactions between the two groups were peaceful. Both parties were thankful for the opportunity to trade with one another. American Indians offered fresh food, horses, and guidance. In exchange, the overlanders gave them their worn-out oxen, clothing, buttons, firearms, and whiskey.

The pioneers often first met American Indians on the Great Plains. The Great Plains are the flat grasslands that stretch from the Missouri River to the Rocky Mountains. The Plains tribes included the Sioux, Apache, Cheyenne, Arapaho, Blackfeet, and Pawnee. The nomadic Plains tribes moved from place to place, following the herds of bison. Bison are large animals with shaggy, brown coats and short horns. Back in the days of the settlers, people called American bison "buffalo." The wild,

▲ The buffalo, or bison, were a major source of food and clothing for the Plains Indians, as well as for the emigrants heading west. Sadly, the bison were hunted almost to the point of extinction.

ox-like animals reminded the Europeans of buffalo from the Old World. Bison was a mainstay of the Plains Indians' diet. The Plains Indians were skilled horsemen, able to kill buffalo with spears. To preserve the meat, they dried it and cut it into strips to make jerky. They produced robes, blankets, and tents from buffalo hides. Using buffalo parts, they created thread, rope, string, glue, and bags to carry water. Buffalo chips were used as fuel for their fires.

Plains Indians

Their villages were always on the move. Their homes had to be easy to take down, transport, and reassemble. The Plains Indians lived in tent-like lodges, or tepees, made of animal hides stretched over a frame of branches. When it was time to move along, they hauled their belongings behind them on carts called travois. A travois is a frame made from a buffalo hide platform stretched between two poles. Ponies pulled the travois to the next village site. Even dogs pulled small travois along behind them.

The Sioux intrigued Francis Parkman, who traveled west on the Oregon Trail in 1846. He spent three weeks living among them and even accompanied them on a buffalo hunt. Parkman made note of how the tribe depended on hunting the buffalo. About the western Sioux, he wrote,

Francis Parkman, The Oregon Trail - Microsoft Internet Explorer

File   Edit   View   Favorites   Tools   Help   Links ″

Address http://xroads.virginia.edu/~HYPER/OREGON/oregon.html

THE OREGON TRAIL
Sketches of Prairie
and Rocky-Mountain Life
by
Francis Parkman

Table of Contents

The Oregon Trail: Sketches of Prairie and Rocky Mountain Life

The Oregon Trail was written by Francis Parkman and published in 1849. The book was an account of his travels along the Oregon Trail, a journey that began as a way to improve his health, as well as an opportunity to study the Plains Indians.

Access this Web site from http://www.myreportlinks.com

"When the buffalo are extinct, they too must dwindle away."[1] Sadly, his words would prove all too true. By the late 1840s, many thousands of pioneers were traveling the trail each year. The herds of buffalo provided the overland travelers with a source of fresh meat. The settlers also killed the huge animals for sport. Sometimes they would cut out just their tongues and leave the rest to rot in the sun. Buffalo tongue was considered a great delicacy. The emigrants' oxen, horses, and mules overgrazed the land. This left less grass for the millions of buffalo. As the number of overland travelers grew larger, the herds of buffalo grew smaller. The herds were so plentiful, the pioneers never dreamed they would soon disappear. Today there are fewer than twenty-five thousand American bison.

The American Indians grew concerned with the growing number of overland travelers. The settlers were threatening their food source and their way of life. Some Plains Indians began demanding tribute from emigrants crossing over their land. Others operated toll bridges. Some emigrants paid the tolls, happy to gain safe passage. Some refused to pay and took their chances. Some American Indians turned to stealing horse and cattle from the emigrants. Stories of Indian attacks, usually highly exaggerated, scared the pioneers. They passed along many tales of American Indians sneaking up on wagon trains to scalp and murder overlanders. American Indian attacks definitely did occur, but they were scarce. And they were often in reaction to bad behavior from the emigrants. The emigrants carried their firearms not just for hunting, but for protection. Many fearful settlers distrusted all American Indians, no matter what tribe they belonged to.

▶ The Civilized and the Savage

It was never likely that the emigrants and the tribes could live peacefully side by side. After all, the emigrants were there to settle the land. The Americans felt they had a right to North America.

If they did not take it, Great Britain would. Neither the British nor the Americans considered that the tribes really owned the land. The way the American Indians and the settlers lived was very different. It was hard for the two to understand one another. The clothes they wore, the buildings they lived in, their languages, their religions: all these things were unalike. The emigrants thought the American Indians' way of life was simple and primitive. The emigrants often referred to the American Indians as savages. The word savage

▲ *This Chinook man is standing along the Columbia River valley. The lifestyle of the natives of the Pacific Northwest was very different from that of the emigrants.*

means wild, uncivilized, and crude. In contrast, Americans considered themselves to be civilized people. They believed American culture was more highly developed and therefore better than the Indian's culture.

▶ Converting the Natives

Some American Christians believed they had a duty to share the teachings of Christ with the Indians. Both Catholics and Protestants sent missionaries to the tribes. The missionaries taught the Indians about Christian beliefs. They also brought many other aspects of American culture to the tribes. They taught them to plant crops and raise livestock. Despite the missionaries' good intentions, American Indians did not always benefit from the missions. Their own traditions, passed down through generations for centuries, were cast aside. Missionaries also unknowingly brought about the deaths of many American Indians by exposing the tribes to fatal diseases like smallpox and measles.

Fur trappers, on the other hand, often imitated the American Indians' way of life. They learned from American Indians the best routes and hunting grounds. Trappers lived in tents. They dressed in deerskin jackets, leggings, and moccasins. Some married American Indian women. The settlers called these men French Indians, because many of them were French Canadian. By the time the emigrants began traveling west, they occasionally hired an Indian to lead them. Other emigrants were less humane. They captured Indians and forced them to act as guides, against their will and without pay.[2]

By the 1850s, relations between the emigrants and the American Indians had turned sour. Two brutal massacres occurred in 1854. In the first, hungry Sioux Indians shot and ate a cow that had wandered into their camp. The cow had belonged to a passing group of Mormons. The Mormons told soldiers at Fort Laramie that the cow had been stolen. A small group of soldiers

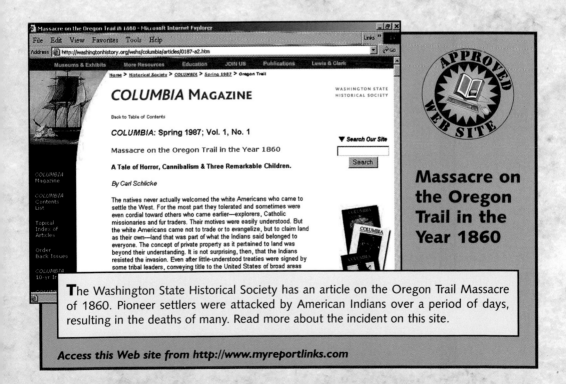

The Washington State Historical Society has an article on the Oregon Trail Massacre of 1860. Pioneer settlers were attacked by American Indians over a period of days, resulting in the deaths of many. Read more about the incident on this site.

Access this Web site from http://www.myreportlinks.com

went out to the Sioux camp. The Sioux refused to hand over the person who had shot the cow. The hot-headed leader of these soldiers, Lieutenant John L. Grattan, fired into the crowd. The Sioux chief had been shot. The Sioux counterattacked and killed every last soldier.[3]

Battle of Blue Water

The second massacre occurred farther west on the trail, near Fort Boise in present-day Idaho. A fight broke out between a group of twenty emigrants and some Yakima Indians. In the end, all twenty of the emigrants, including women and children, were dead. The Yakima fled with the emigrants' money and cattle.[4]

Emigrants felt the United States should protect them from such American Indian attacks. The next spring, only five hundred people headed west to Oregon. The United States Army decided it needed a show of force to put the American Indians in their place. A group of six hundred soldiers marched west from Fort Leavenworth, Missouri. When they reached a popular campsite called Ash Hollow, they came across a group of Sioux Indians. Some soldiers spoke with the Sioux while others sneaked up from behind. The soldiers killed eighty-six Sioux, including many women and children. They took another forty women and children prisoner. Only four American soldiers

▲ Chief Joseph was the leader of the Nez Percé Indians. He became famous for the way he surrendered with dignity after a spirited resistance.

died. This fight became known as the Battle of Blue Water, or the Battle of Ash Hollow. After this, both sides assumed the worst of each other and were quick to react with violence. It sparked the Indian Wars that would last until the 1890s.

▶ I Will Fight No More Forever

The Nez Percé Indians lived in the Pacific Northwest. In 1877, the United States Army tried to force them onto a small reservation. Not everyone went peacefully. About one quarter of the people refused to go. A small group of outraged Nez Percé warriors retaliated. They attacked a group of American settlers. The United States Army decided to solve the problem with military force. Three hundred and fifty Nez Percé ran for their lives. They fled for 1,300 miles through the mountains toward Canada. Before they reached their destination, they surrendered. Their leader, Chief Joseph, was unable to watch his people run while starving, cold, and exhausted. His words upon surrender have become famous: "Here me, my chiefs! I am tired. My heart is sick and sad. From where the sun now stands I will fight no more forever."[5]

▶ Lessons From the Past

Today the Oregon Trail is a National Historic Trail. History buffs can follow the general course of the trail in their cars. They can see Independence

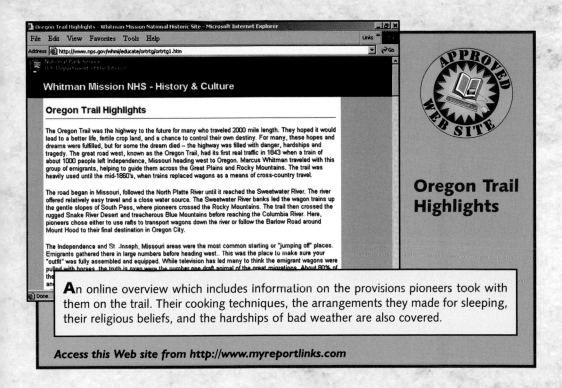

Whitman Mission NHS - History & Culture

Oregon Trail Highlights

The Oregon Trail was the highway to the future for many who traveled 2000 mile length. They hoped it would lead to a better life, fertile crop land, and a chance to control their own destiny. For many, these hopes and dreams were fulfilled, but for some the dream died – the highway was filled with danger, hardships and tragedy. The great road west, known as the Oregon Trail, had its first real traffic in 1843 when a train of about 1000 people left Independence, Missouri heading west to Oregon. Marcus Whitman traveled with this group of emigrants, helping to guide them across the Great Plains and Rocky Mountains. The trail was heavily used until the mid-1860's, when trains replaced wagons as a means of cross-country travel.

The road began in Missouri, followed the North Platte River until it reached the Sweetwater River. The river offered relatively easy travel and a close water source. The Sweetwater River banks led the wagon trains up the gentle slopes of South Pass, where pioneers crossed the Rocky Mountains. The trail then crossed the rugged Snake River Desert and treacherous Blue Mountains before reaching the Columbia River. Here, pioneers chose either to use rafts to transport wagons down the river or follow the Barlow Road around Mount Hood to their final destination in Oregon City.

The Independence and St. Joseph, Missouri areas were the most common starting or "jumping off" places. Emigrants gathered there in large numbers before heading west.. This was the place to make sure your "outfit" was fully assembled and equipped. While television has led many to think the emigrant wagons were pulled with horses, the truth is oxen were the number one draft animal of the great migrations. About 80% of

Oregon Trail Highlights

An online overview which includes information on the provisions pioneers took with them on the trail. Their cooking techniques, the arrangements they made for sleeping, their religious beliefs, and the hardships of bad weather are also covered.

Access this Web site from http://www.myreportlinks.com

Rock carved with the names of pioneers. Chimney Rock still towers over the prairie for all to wonder at. Less remains of the actual trail itself, though 300 miles of wagon ruts are still visible. The trail, once a path through the wilderness, is now largely settled. While the trail itself is a thing of the past, people are working to tell the story of this saga of American history. Museums, trail markers, and historic monuments keep the memory of the pioneers and their prairie schooners alive. They help modern-day Americans understand the courage and daring of the overland settlers.

Report Links

The Internet sites described below can be accessed at http://www.myreportlinks.com

▶**Oregon National Historic Trail**
Editor's Choice This is the National Park Service's Web site for the 2,170-mile long Oregon Trail.

▶**End of the Oregon Trail Interpretive Center**
Editor's Choice Learn about the Oregon Trail from this site.

▶**Discoverers and Explorers**
Editor's Choice At this site, you will learn about some Oregonian trailblazers.

▶**NebraskaStudies.org: The Oregon Trail**
Editor's Choice This is a comprehensive site detailing the Oregon Trail and Nebraska.

▶**Lewis and Clark**
Editor's Choice Visit this PBS site to learn more about Lewis and Clark.

▶**Whitman Mission National Historic Site**
Editor's Choice This NPS Web site commemorates missionaries Marcus and Narcissa Whitman.

▶**American Indians of the Pacific Northwest**
This is the Web site for the American Indian Relief Council (AIRC).

▶**American Prophet: The Story of Joseph Smith**
This PBS Web site looks at the life of Joseph Smith.

▶**Brigham Young**
An examination of the life of Brigham Young.

▶**Christopher Columbus**
The Mariners' Museum presents this look at the life of Christopher Columbus.

▶**The Donner Party**
PBS presents the story of the Donner Party on this Web site.

▶**Ferdinand Magellan's Voyage Round the World, 1519–1522 CE**
Learn about Ferdinand Magellan and his famous trip from information on this site.

▶**The Frontier in American History**
On this site, learn how frontier life defined the United States.

▶**George Vancouver**
Read about George Vancouver and his accomplishments from this online resource.

▶**Golden Spike National Historic Site**
This National Park Service site gives an overview of the Golden Spike National Historic Park.

Report Links

The Internet sites described below can be accessed at
http://www.myreportlinks.com

▶**Guide to the Photographs of Ezra Meeker**
Photos and facts on an Oregon Trailblazer can be found on this Washington University site.

▶**John Jacob Astor: A Self-Invented Money-Making Machine**
Learn more about John Jacob Astor from this article.

▶**The Journey by Land**
Take a look at a map and overview of the Oregon Trail system.

▶**Life and Death on the Oregon Trail**
Read about the country's longest graveyard.

▶**Manifest Destiny**
An in-depth look at Manifest Destiny is available on this site.

▶**Massacre on the Oregon Trail in the Year 1860**
Learn about the worst clash between settlers and American Indians on the trail.

▶**The Oregon Territory and Its Pioneers**
This site offers information on westward migration during the 1800s.

▶**The Oregon Trail**
This is the Idaho State University Web site for the Oregon Trail.

▶**Oregon Trail Highlights**
Read this National Park Service article on the Oregon Trail.

▶***The Oregon Trail: Sketches of Prairie and Rocky Mountain Life***
A full-text version of *The Oregon Trail* is available on this Web site.

▶**Oregon Trail: Wagon Tracks West**
This article offers insight into the great westward migration.

▶**The People . . . Native Americans**
View the Library of Congress' online resources for American Indian culture.

▶**Pioneer and Emigrant Women**
Biographies and genealogical information of pioneer women are available here.

▶**Transcontinental Railroad**
Learn more about the construction of the first transcontinental railroad in the United States.

▶**Wandering the West**
This is a collection of historical articles originally published in *The Tombstone Epitaph*.

alkali—Describing water or soil poisoned with high levels of caustic mineral salts.

axle—A bar or shaft that allows wheels to revolve.

buffalo chips—The dried dung of bison, used for campfire fuel by the pioneers.

buckskin—The tanned hide of deer, used by American Indians for clothing.

burlap—A coarsely woven cloth often used for bags.

captain—The elected leader of a wagon train.

embargo—A law that forbids trade.

emigrants—People who leave their country to settle elsewhere.

forty-niners—People who went west in search of gold; named after the year that the first wave of gold diggers went west.

frontier—The border or region that marks the end of settled territory.

jumping-off point—The place from which a person or group of people begin a journey. This is sometimes also called a terminus.

Manifest Destiny—A movement and policy whose believers pushed for the expansion of the borders of the United States to span from the Atlantic to Pacific oceans. Believers in Manifest Destiny felt this goal was inevitable.

migration—The act of moving from one area to settle in another.

Mormon—A person who belongs to the Church of Jesus Christ of Latter-day Saints.

mule—A cross between a donkey and a horse; an animal known for its strength, hardiness, and stubborn nature.

nomad—A person who roams from place to place.

ox (pl. oxen)—A strong animal used by people to pull heavy loads.

pilot—A person who guided emigrants through the American West.

pioneer—An adventurer who is one of the first people to attempt something new.

prairie—A stretch of treeless grassland.

rendezvous—A place that has been agreed to as a meeting point. In the American West, a rendezvous was where trappers would meet to sell or trade their pelts.

reservation—Land set aside by the government for American Indians.

sailcloth—Either a heavy canvas used for such things as sails and tents, or a light canvas used for items of clothing such as bonnets.

saleratus—Sodium bicarbonate, or baking soda; used to make bread rise.

sentry—A lookout; one who watched over the safety of the camp and animals.

sutler—The merchant or storekeeper at a frontier fort.

tepee—An American Indian building made of hides stretched over a pole frame.

travois—A kind of cart used by American Indians; a buffalo hide frame on two poles dragged behind a horse, person, or dog.

Chapter 1. Trials and Adventures of the Pioneers

1. David Klausmeyer, ed., *Oregon Trail Stories: True Accounts of Life in a Covered Wagon* (Guilford, Conn.: TwoDot, 2004), pp. 16–17.

2. David Dary, *The Oregon Trail* (New York: Alfred A. Knopf, 2004), p. 178.

3. Ibid., p. 179.

4. Kristin Johnson, ed., *"Unfortunate Emigrants"*: *Narratives of the Donner Party* (Logan: Utah State University Press, 1996), p. 292.

5. Ibid., p. 150.

6. Ibid., p. 131.

Chapter 2. Early Days of the Oregon Country

1. Lillian Schlissel, *Women's Diaries of the Westward Journey* (New York: Schocken Books, 1992), p. 19.

2. David Dary, *The Oregon Trail* (New York: Alfred A. Knopf, 2004), p. 7.

3. Ibid., p. 9.

4. Robert V. Hine and John Mack Faragher, *The American West: A New Interpretive History* (New Haven: Yale University Press, 2000), p. 186.

Chapter 3. Setting Out for the Frontier

1. John D. Unruh, Jr., *The Plains Across: The Overland Emigrants and the Trans-Mississippi West, 1840–60* (Champaign: University of Illinois Press, 1979), p. 91.

2. David Klausmeyer, ed., *Oregon Trail Stories: True Accounts of Life in a Covered Wagon* (Guilford, Conn.: TwoDot, 2004), p. 129.

3. Laura Ingalls Wilder, *Little House on the Prairie* (New York: Harper Trophy, 1971), p. 106.

4. Kenneth L. Holmes and David C. Duniway, eds., *Covered Wagon Women: Diaries and Letters from the Western Trails, 1852, Vol. 5 The Oregon Trail* (Lincoln: University of Nebraska Press, 1986), p. 95.

5. Ibid., p. 62.

Chapter 4. Oregon Fever— "Oregon or Bust!"

1. Kenneth L. Holmes and David C. Duniway, eds., *Covered Wagon Women: Diaries and Letters from the Western Trails, 1852, Vol. 5 The Oregon Trail* (Lincoln: University of Nebraska Press, 1986), pp. 108–109.

2. John D. Unruh, Jr., *The Plains Across: The Overland Emigrants and the Trans-Mississippi West, 1840–60* (Champaign: University of Illinois Press, 1979), p. 408.

3. Renee Rusler, "Oregon Trail Highlights," *Whitman Mission NHS: History and Culture,* January 31, 2004, <http://www.nps.gov/whmi/educate/ortrtg/ortrtg1.htm> (January 25, 2006).

4. Holmes and Duniway, p. 65.

5. Ibid., p. 282.

Chapter 5. Famous People of the Oregon Trail

1. John D. Unruh, Jr., *The Plains Across: The Overland Emigrants and the Trans-Mississippi West, 1840–60* (Champaign: University of Illinois Press, 1979), p. 294.

2. Laton McCartney, *Across the Great Divide: Robert Stuart and the Discovery of the Oregon Trail* (New York: Free Press, 2003), p. 151.

3. Ibid., p. 222.

4. David Dary, *The Oregon Trail* (New York: Alfred A. Knopf, 2004), p. 64.

Chapter 6. Impact of the Oregon Trail

1. Francis Parkman, *The Oregon Trail* (Washington, D.C.: National Geographic Society, 2002), p. 108.

2. John D. Unruh, Jr., *The Plains Across: The Overland Emigrants and the Trans-Mississippi West, 1840–60* (Champaign: University of Illinois Press, 1979), p. 157.

3. Peter M. Chaitin, et. al, *Story of the Great American West* (Pleasantville, N.Y.: Reader's Digest Association, 1977), p. 211.

4. David Dary, *The Oregon Trail* (New York: Alfred A. Knopf, 2004), pp. 260–261.

5. The West Film Project, "Chief Joseph," *PBS-The West,* 2001, <http://www.pbs.org/weta/thewest/people/a_c/chiefjoseph.htm> (January 26, 2006).

O'Brien, Mary Barmeyer. *Into the Western Winds: Pioneer Boys Traveling the Overland Trails.* Guilford, Conn.: Globe Pequot Press, 2003.

Blackwood, Gary L. *Life on the Oregon Trail.* San Diego, Calif.: Lucent Books, Inc., 1999.

Blashfield, Jean F. *The Oregon Trail.* Minneapolis, Minn.: Compass Point Books, 2001.

Gregory, Kristiana. *Across the Wide and Lonesome Prairie: The Oregon Trail Diary of Hattie Campbell, 1847.* New York: Scholastic, 1997.

Gunderson, Mary. *Oregon Trail Cooking.* Mankato, Minn.: Blue Earth Books, 2000.

Harness, Cheryl. *The Tragic Tale of Narcissa Whitman and a Faithful History of the Oregon Trail.* Washington, D.C.: National Geographic Society, 2006.

Jaffe, Elizabeth D. *The Oregon Trail.* Mankato, Minn.: Bridgestone Books, 2002.

Levine, Ellen. *The Journal of Jebediah Barstow, an Emigrant on the Oregon Trail: Overland 1845.* New York: Scholastic, 2002.

Moeller, Bill and Jan. *The Oregon Trail: A Photographic Journey.* Missoula, Mont.: Mountain Press Publishing Co., 2001.

Olson, Steven P. *The Oregon Trail: A Primary Source History of the Route to the American West.* New York: Rosen Central, 2004.

Rau, Dana Meachen. *The Life on the Oregon Trail.* San Diego, Calif.: Kidhaven Press, 2002.

Steele, Christy, ed., with Ann Hodgson. *A Covered Wagon Girl: The Diary of Sallie Hester, 1849–1850.* Mankato, Minn.: Blue Earth Books, 2000.